GEORGE S. CLASON

THE RICHEST MAN IN BABYLON: WITH THE MAGIC STORY

FREDERICK VAN RENSSELAER DEY

The Richest Man in Babylon

George S. Clason

CONTENTS

The Tale of The Man Who Desired Much Gold

BANSIR, the chariot builder of Babylon, was thoroughly discouraged. From his seat upon the low wall surrounding his property, he gazed sadly at his simple home and the open work shop in which stood a partially completed chariot.

His wife frequently appeared at the open door. Her furtive glances in his direction reminded him that the meal bag was almost empty and he should be at work finishing the chariot, hammering and hewing, polishing and painting, stretching taut the leather over the wheel rims, preparing it for delivery so he could collect from his wealthy customer.

Nevertheless, his fat, muscular body sat stolidly upon the wall. His slow mind was struggling patiently with a problem for which he could find no answer. The hot, tropical sun, so typical of this valley of the Euphrates, beat down upon him mercilessly. Beads of perspiration formed upon his brow and trickled down unnoticed to lose themselves in the hairy jungle on his chest.

Beyond his home towered the high terraced walls surrounding the king's palace. Nearby, cleaving the blue heavens, was the painted tower to the Temple of Bel. In the shadow of such grandeur was his simple home and many others far less neat and well cared for. Babylon was like this - a mixture of grandeur and squalor, of dazzling wealth and direst poverty, crowded together without plan or system within the protecting walls of the city.

Behind him, had he cared to turn and look, the noisy chariots of the rich, jostled and crowded aside the sandaled tradesmen as well as the barefooted beggars. Even the rich, in turn, were forced to turn into the gutters to clear the way for the long lines of slave water carriers, on the "King's Business", each bearing a heavy goat skin of water to be poured upon the hanging gardens.

Bansir was too engrossed in his own problem to hear or heed the confused hubub of the busy city. It was the unexpected twanging of the strings from a familiar lyre that aroused him from his reverie. He turned and looked into the sensitive, smiling face of his best friend - Kobbi, the musician.

"May God bless thee with great liberality, my good friend", began Kobbi with an elaborate salute. "Yet, it does appear he hath have already been so generous thou needest not to labor. I rejoice with thee in thy good fortune. More, I would even share it with thee. Pray, from thy purse which must be bulging else thou wouldst be busy in yon shop, extract but two humble shekels and lend them to me until after the noblemen's feast this night. Thou wilt not miss them ere they are returned."

"If I did have two shekels", Bansir responded gloomily, "to no one could I lend them - not even to you, my best of friends; for they would be my fortune - my entire fortune. No one lends his entire fortune, not even to his best friend."

"What!" exclaimed Kobbi with genuine surprise, 'Thou hast not one shekel in thy purse, yet sit like a statue upon a wall! Why not complete that chariot? How else canst thou provide for thy noble appetite? Tis not like thee, my friend. Where is thy endless energy? Doth something distress thee? Has God brought to thee troubles?"

"A torment from God it must be," Bansir agreed. "It began with a dream, a senseless dream, in which I thought I was a man of means. From my belt hung a handsome purse, heavy with coins. There were shekels which I cast with careless freedom to the beggars; there were pieces of silver with which I did buy finery for my wife and whatever I did desire for myself; there were pieces of gold which made me feel assured of the future and unafraid to spend the silver. A glorious feeling of contentment was within me! You would not have known me for thy hard working friend. Nor wouldst have known my wife, so free from wrinkles was her face and shining with happiness. She was again the smiling maiden of our early married days."

"A pleasant dream, indeed," commented Kobbi, "but why should such pleasant feelings as it aroused turn thee into a glum statue upon the wall?"

"Why, indeed! Because when I awoke and remembered how empty was my purse, a feeling of rebellion swept over me. Let us talk it over together, for, as the sailors do say, we ride in the same boat, we two. As youngsters, we went together to the priests to learn wisdom. As young men, we shared each other's pleasures. As grown men, we have always been close friends. We have been contented subjects of our king. We have been satisfied to work long hours and spend our earnings freely. We have earned much coin in the years that have passed, yet to know the joys that come from wealth, we must dream about them. Bah! Are we more than dumb sheep? We live in the richest city in all the world. The travelers do say none equals it in wealth. About us is much display of wealth, but of it we ourselves have naught. After half a lifetime of hard labor, thou, my best of friends, has an empty purse and sayest to me, 'May I borrow such a trifle as two shekels until after the noblemen's feast this night'? Then, what do I reply? Do I say here is my purse; its contents will I gladly share? No, I admit that my purse is as empty as thine. What is the matter? Why cannot we acquire silver and gold - more than enough for food and robes?

"Consider, also, our sons," Bansir continued, "are they not following in the footsteps of their fathers? Need they and their families and their sons and their sons' families live all their lives in the midst of such treasures of gold, and yet, like us, be content to banquet upon sour goat's milk and porridge?"

"Never, in all the years of our friendship,didst talk like this before, Bansir." Kobbi was puzzled.

"Never in all those years did I think like this before. From early dawn until darkness stopped me, I have labored to build the finest chariots any man could make, softheartedly hoping some day God would recognize my worthy deeds and bestow upon me great prosperity. This he has never done. At last, I realize this he will never do. Therefore, my heart is sad. I wish to be a man of means. I wish to own lands and cattle, to have fine robes and coins in my purse. I am willing to work for these things with all the strength in my back, with all the skill in my hands, with all the cunning in my mind, but I wish my labors to be fairly rewarded. What is the matter with us? Again I ask you! Why cannot we have our just share of the good things so plentiful or those who have the gold with which to buy them?"

"Would I knew an answer!" Kobbi replied. "No better than thou am I satisfied. My earnings from my lyre are quickly gone. Often must I plan and scheme that my family be not hungry. Also, within my breast is a deep longing for a lyre large enough that it may truly sing the strains of music that do surge through my mind. With such an instrument could I make music finer than even the king has heard before."

"Such a lyre thou shouldst have. No man in all Babylon could make it sing more sweetly; could make it sing so sweetly, not only the king but God himself would be delighted. But how mayest thou secure it while we both of us are as poor as the king's slaves. Listen to the bell! Here they come." He pointed to the long column of half naked, sweating water bearers plodding laboriously up the narrow street from the river. Five abreast they marched, each bent under a heavy goatskin of water.

"A fine figure of a man, he who doth lead them." Kobbi indicated the wearer of the bell who marched in front without a load. "A prominent man in his own country, 'tis easy to see."

"There are many good figures in the line," Bansir agreed, "as good men as we. Tall, blond men from the north, laughing black men from the south, little brown men from the nearer countries. All marching together from the river to the gardens, back and forth, day after day, year after year. Naught of happiness to look forward to. Beds of straw upon which to sleep hard grain porridge to eat. Pity the poor brutes, Kobbi!"

"Pity them I do. Yet, thou dost make me see how little better off are we, free men though we call ourselves."

'That is truth, Kobbi, unpleasant thought, though it be. We do not wish to go on year after year living slavish lives. Working, working, working! Getting nowhere."

"Might we not find out how others acquire gold and do as they do?" Kobbi inquired.

"Perhaps there is some secret we might learn if we but sought from those who knew," replied Bansir thoughtfully.

"'This very day," suggested Kobbi, "I did pass our old friend, Arkad, riding in his golden chariot. This, I will say, he did not look over my humble head as many in his station might consider his right. Instead, he did wave his hand that all onlookers might see him pay greetings and bestow his smile of friendship on his friend Kobbi, the musician."

"'He is claimed to be the richest man in all Babylon," Bansir mused.

"So rich, the king is said to seek his golden aid in affairs of the treasury," Kobbi replied.

"So rich," Bansir interrupted, "I fear if I should meet him in the darkness of the night, I should lay my hands upon his fat wallet."

"Nonsense," reproved Kobbi, "a man's wealth is not in the purse he carries. A fat purse quickly empties if there be no golden stream to refill it. Arkad has an income that constantly keeps his purse full, no matter how liberally he spends."

"Income, that is the thing," ejaculated Bansir: "I wish an income that will keep flowing into my purse whether I sit upon the wall or travel to far lands. Arkad must know how a man can make an income for himself. Dost suppose it is something he could make clear to a mind as slow as mine?"

"Methinks, he did teach his knowledge to his son, Nomasir," Kobbi responded. "Did he not go to Nineveh and, so it is told at the inn, become without aid from his father, one of the richest men in that city?"

"Kobbi, thou bringest to me a rare thought." A new light gleamed in Bansir's eyes. "It costs nothing to ask wise advice from a good friend and Arkad was always that. Never mind though our purses be as empty as the falcon's nest of a year ago. Let that not detain us. We are weary of being without gold in the midst of plenty. We wish to become men of means. Come, let us go to Arkad and ask how we, also, may acquire incomes for ourselves."

'Thou speakest with true inspiration, Bansir. Thou bringeth to my mind a new understanding. Thou makest me to realize the reason why we have never found any measure of wealth. We never sought it. Thou labored patiently to build the staunchest chariots in Babylon. To that purpose was devoted your best endeavors. Therefore, at it thou didst succeed. I strove to become a skilful lyre player. And, at it I did succeed."

"In those things toward which we exerted our best endeavors we succeeded. God was content to let us continue thus. Now, at last, we see a light bright like that from the rising sun. It biddeth us to learn more that we may prosper more. 'Tis the wisest thing we have ever done. With a new understanding we shall find honorable ways to accomplish our desires."

"Let us go to Arkad this very day," Bansir urged. "Also, let us ask other friends of our boyhood days, who have fared no better than ourselves, to join us that they, too, may share in his wisdom".

"Thou-wert ever thus thoughtful of thy friends, Bansir. Therefore, hast thou many friends. It shall be as thou sayest. We go this day and take them with us."

THE RICHEST MAN IN BABYLON TELLS HIS SYSTEM

IN Old Babylon there once lived a certain very rich man named Arkad. Far and wide he was famed for his great wealth. Also was he famed for his liberality. He was generous in his charities. He was generous with his family. He was liberal in his own expenses. But nevertheless each year his wealth increased more rapidly than he spent it.

And there were certain friends of younger days who came to him and said: "You, Arkad, are more fortunate than we. You have become the richest man in all Babylon while we struggle for existence. You can wear the finest garments and you can enjoy the rarest foods, while we must be content if we can clothe our families in raiment that is presentable and feed them as best we can.

"Yet, once we were equal. We studied under the same master. We played in the same games. And in neither the studies nor the games did you outshine us. And in the years since, you have been no more an honorable citizen than we.

"Nor, have you worked harder or more faithfully, in so far as we can judge. Why, then, should a fickle fate single you out to enjoy all the good things of life and ignore us who are equally deserving?"

Thereupon Arkad remonstrated with them, saying, "If you have not acquired more than a bare existence in the years since we were youths, it is because you either have failed to learn the laws that govern the building of wealth, or else you do not observe them.

"'Fickle fate' is a vicious goddess that brings no permanent good to anyone. On the contrary she brings ruin to almost every man upon whom she showers unearned gold. She makes wanton spenders, who soon dissipate all they receive and are left beset by overwhelming appetites and desires they have not the ability to gratify. Yet others whom she favors become misers and hoard their wealth, fearing to spend what they have, knowing they do not possess the ability to replace it. They further are beset by fear of robbers and doom themselves to lives of emptiness and secret misery.

"Others, there probably are, who can take unearned gold and add to it and continue to be happy and contented citizens. But so few are they, I know of them but by hearsay. Think you of the men who have inherited sudden wealth, and see if these things are not so."

His friends admitted that of the men they knew who had inherited wealth these words were true, and they besought him to explain to them how he had become possessed of so much property, so he continued:

"In my youth I looked about me and saw all the good things there were to bring happiness and contentment. And I realized that wealth increased the potency of all these.

"Wealth is a power. With wealth many things are possible.

"One may ornament the home with the richest of furnishings.

"One may sail the distant seas.

"One may feast on the delicacies of far lands.

"One may buy the ornaments of the gold worker and the stone polisher.

"One may even build mighty temples for God.

"One may do all these things and many others in which there is delight for the senses and gratification for the soul.

"And when I realized all this I declared to myself that I would claim my share of the good things of life. I would not be one of those who stand afar off, enviously watching others enjoy. I would not be content to clothe myself in the cheapest raiment that looked respectable. I would not be satisfied with the lot of a poor man. On the contrary, I would make myself a guest at this banquet of good things.

"Being, as you know, the son of a humble merchant, one of a large family with no hope of an inheritance, and not being endowed, as you have so frankly said, with superior powers or wisdom, I decided that if I was to achieve what I desired, time and study would be required.

"As for time, all men have it in abundance. You, each of you, have let slip by sufficient to have made yourselves wealthy. Yet, you admit you have nothing to show except your good families, of which you can be justly proud.

"As for study, did not our wise teacher teach us that learning was of two kinds: the one kind being the things we learned and knew, and the other being in the training that taught us how to find out what we did not know?

"Therefore, did I decide to find out how one might accumulate wealth, and when I had found out, to make this my task and do it well. For, is it not wise that we should enjoy while we dwell in the brightness of the sunshine, for sorrows enough shall descend upon us when we depart for the darkness of the world of spirit?

"I found employment as a scribe in the hall of records, and long hours each day I labored upon the clay tablets. Week after week, and month after month, I labored, yet for my earnings I had naught to show. Food and clothing and penance to God, and other things of which I could remember not what, absorbed all my earnings. But my determination did not leave me.

"And one day Algamish, the money lender, came to the house of the city master and ordered a copy of the Ninth Law, and he said to me, 'I must have this in two days, and if the task is done by that time, two coppers will I give to thee.'

"So I labored hard, but the law was long, and when Algamish returned the task was unfinished. He was angry, and had I been his slave he would have beaten me. But knowing the city master would not permit him to injure me, I was unafraid, so I said to him:

"'Algamish, you are a very rich man. Tell me how I may also become rich, and all night I will carve upon the clay, and when the sun rises it shall be completed.'

"He smiled at me and replied, 'You are a forward knave, but we will call it a bargain.'

"All that night I carved, though my back pained and the smell of the wick made my head ache until my eyes could hardly see. But when he returned at sunup the tablets were complete.

"'Now,' I said, 'tell me what you promised.'

"'You have fulfilled your part of our bargain, my son,' he said to me kindly, 'and I am ready to fulfill mine. I will tell you these things you wish to know because I am becoming an old man, and an old tongue loves to wag. And when youth comes to age for advice he receives the wisdom of years. But too often does youth think that age knows only the wisdom of days that are gone, and therefore profits not. But remember this, the sun that shines today is the sun that shone when thy father was born, and will still be shining when thy last grandchild shall pass into the darkness.

"'The thoughts of youth,' he continued, 'are bright things that shine forth like the meteors that oft make brilliant the sky, but the wisdom of age is like the fixed stars that shine so unchanged that the sailor may depend upon them to steer his course.

"'Mark you well my words, for if you do not you will fail to grasp the truth that I will tell you, and you will think that your night's work has been in vain.'

"Then he looked at me shrewdly from under his shaggy brows and said in a low, forceful tone, 'I found the road to wealth when I decided that a part of all I earned was mine to keep. And so will you.'

"Then he continued to look at me with a glance that I could feel pierce me but said no more.

"'Is that all?' I asked.

"That was sufficient to change the heart of a sheep herder into the heart of a money lender,' he replied.

"'But all I earn is mine to keep, is it not? I demanded.

"'Far from it,' he replied. 'Do you not pay the garment-maker? Do you not pay the sandal-maker? Do you not pay for the things you eat? Can you live in Babylon without spending? What have you to show for your earnings of the past month? What for the past year? Fool! You pay to everyone but yourself. Dullard, you labor for others. As well be a slave and work for what your master gives you to eat and wear. If you did keep for yourself one-tenth of all you earn, how much would you have in ten years?'

"My knowledge of the numbers did not forsake me, and I answered, 'As much as I earn in one year.'

"'You speak but half the truth, he retorted. 'Every gold piece you save is a slave to work for you. Every copper it earns is its child that also can earn for you. If you would become wealthy, then what you save must earn, and its children must earn, and its children's children must earn, that all may help to give to you the abundance you crave.

"'You think I cheat you for your long night's work,' he continued, 'but I am paying you a thousand times over if you have the intelligence to grasp the truth I offer you.

"'A PART OF ALL YOU EARN IS YOURS TO KEEP. It should not be less than a tenth no matter how little you earn. It can be as much more as you can afford. Pay yourself first. Do not buy from the cloth maker and the sandal maker more than you can pay out of the rest and still have enough for food and charity and penance to God.

"'Wealth, like a tree, grows from a tiny seed. The first copper you save is the seed from which your tree of wealth shall grow. The sooner you plant that seed the sooner shall the tree grow. And the more faithfully you nourish and water that tree with consistent savings, the sooner may you bask in contentment beneath its shade.' So saying, he took his tablets and went away.

"I thought much about what he had said to me, and it seemed reasonable. So I decided that I would try it. Each time I was paid I took one from each ten pieces of copper and hid it away. And strange as it may seem, I was no shorter of funds than before. I noticed little difference as I managed to get along without it. But often I was tempted as my hoard began to grow, to spend it for some of the good things the merchants displayed, brought by camels and ships from the land of the Phoenicians. But I wisely refrained.

"A twelfth month after Algamish had gone he again returned and said to me, 'Son, have you paid to yourself not less than one tenth of all you have earned for the past year?'

"I answered proudly, 'Yes, master, I have.'

"'That is good,' he answered beaming upon me, 'And what have you done with it?'

"'I have given it to Azmur, the brick maker, who told me he was traveling over the seven seas and in Tyre he would buy for me the rare jewels of the Phoenicians. When he returns we shall sell these at high prices and divide the earnings.'

"'Every fool must learn,' he growled, 'but why trust the knowledge of a brick maker about jewels? Would you go to the bread maker to inquire about the stars? No, by my tunic, you would go to the astrologer, if you had power to think. Your savings are gone, youth, you have jerked your wealth tree up by the roots. But plant another. Try again. And next time if you would have advice about jewels, go to the jewel merchant. If you would know the truth about sheep, go to the herdsman. Advice is one thing that is freely given away, but watch that you take only what is worth having. He who takes advice about his savings from one who is inexperienced in such matters, shall pay with his savings for proving the falsity of their opinions.' Saying this, he went away.

"And it was as he said. For the Phoenicians are scoundrels and sold to Azmur worthless bits of glass that looked like gems. But as Algamish had bid me, I again saved each tenth copper, for I now had formed the habit and it was no longer difficult.

"A twelve months later Algamish again came to the room of the scribes and addressed me. 'What progress have you made since last I saw you?

"'I have paid myself faithfully,' I replied, 'and my savings I have entrusted to Agger the shieldmaker, to buy bronze, and each fourth month he does pay me the rental.'

"That is good. And what do you do with the rental?

"I do have a great feast with honey and fine wine and spiced cake. Also I have bought me a scarlet tunic. And some day I shall buy me a young ass upon which to ride.'

"To which Algamish laughed. 'You do eat the children of your savings. Then how do you expect them to work for you? And how can they have children that will also work for you? First get thee an army of golden slaves and then many a rich banquet may you enjoy without regret.' So saying he again went away.

"Nor did I again see him for two years, when he once more returned and his face was full of deep lines and his eyes drooped, for he was becoming a very old man. And he said to me, "Arkad, hast thou yet achieved the wealth thou dreamed of?'

"And I answered, 'Not yet all that I desire, but some I have and it earns more, and its earnings earn more.'

"'And do you still take the advice of brick makers?'

"'About brick making they give good advice,' I retorted.

"Arkad," he continued, 'you have learned your lessons well. You first learned to live upon less than you could earn. Next you learned to seek advice from those who were competent through their own experiences to give it. And, lastly, you have learned to make gold work for you.

"'You have taught yourself how to acquire money, how to keep it, and how to use it. Therefore, you are competent for a responsible position. I am becoming an old man, my sons think only of spending and give no thought to earning. My interests are great and I fear too much for me to look after. If you will go to Nippur and look after my lands there, I shall make you my partner and you shall share in my estate.'

"So I went to Nippur and took charge of his holdings, which were large. And because I was full of ambition and because I had mastered the three laws of successfully handling wealth, I was enabled to increase greatly the value of his properties. So I prospered much, and when the spirit of Algamish departed for the sphere of darkness, I did share in his estate as he had arranged under the law."

So spake Arkad, and when he had finished his tale, one of his friends said, "You were indeed fortunate that Algamish made of you an heir."

"Fortunate only in that I had the desire to prosper before I first met him. For four years did I not prove my definiteness of purpose by keeping one tenth of all I earned? Would you call a fisherman lucky who for years so studied the habits of the fish that with each changing wind he could cast his nets about them? Opportunity is a haughty goddess who wastes no time with those who are unprepared."

"You had strong will power to keep on after you lost your first year's savings. You are unusual in that way," spoke up another.

"Will power!" retorted Arkad. "What nonsense. Do you think will power gives a man the strength to lift a burden the camel cannot carry, or to draw a load the oxen cannot budge? Will power is but the unflinching purpose to carry a task you set for yourself to fulfillment. If I set for myself a task, be it ever so trifling, I shall see it through. How else shall I have confidence in myself to do important things? Should I say to myself, 'For a hundred days as I walk across the bridge into the city, I will pick from the road a pebble and cast it into the stream,' I would do it. If on the seventh day I passed by without remembering, I would not say to myself, "Tomorrow I will cast two pebbles which will do as well.' Instead, I would retrace my steps and cast the pebble. Nor on the twentieth day would I say to myself, 'Arkad, this is useless. What does it avail you to cast a pebble every day? Throw in a handful and be done with it.' No, I would not say that nor do it. When I set a task for myself, I complete it. Therefore, I am careful not to start difficult and impractical tasks, because I love leisure."

And then another friend spoke up and said, "If what you tell is true, and it does seem as you have said, reasonable, then being so simple, if all men did it, there would not be enough wealth to go around."

"Wealth grows wherever men exert energy," Arkad replied. "If a rich man builds him a new palace, is the gold he pays out gone? No, the brick maker has part of it and the laborer has part of it, and the artist has part of it. And everyone who labors upon the house has part of it. Yet when the palace is completed, is it not worth all it cost? And is the ground upon which it stands not worth more because it is there? And is the ground that adjoins it not worth more because it is there? Wealth grows in magic ways. No man can prophesy the limit of it. Have not the Phoenicians built great cities on barren coasts with the wealth that comes from their ships of commerce on the seas?"

"What then do you advise us to do that we also may become rich?" asked still another of his friends. 'The years have passed and we are no longer young men and we have nothing put by."

"I advise that you take the wisdom of Aglamish and say to yourselves, 'A part of all I earn is mine to keep.' Say it in the morning when you first arise. Say it at noon. Say it at night. Say it each hour of every day. Say it to yourself until the words stand out like letters of fire across the sky.

"Impress yourself with the idea. Fill yourself with the thought. Then take whatever portions seem wise. Let it be not less than one tenth and lay it by. Arrange your other expenditures to do this if necessary. But lay by that portion first. Soon you will realize what a rich feeling it is to have something upon which you alone have claim. As it grows it will stimulate you. A new joy of life will thrill you. Greater efforts will come to you to earn more. For of your increased earnings, will not the same percentage be also yours to keep?

'Then learn to make your treasure work for you. Make it your slave. Make its children and its children's children work for you.

"Insure an income for thy future. Look thou at the aged and forget not that in the days to come thou also will be numbered among them. Therefore invest thy treasure with greatest caution that it be not lost. Usurious rates of return are deceitful sirens that sing but to lure the unwary upon the rocks of loss and remorse.

"Provide also that thy family may not want should God call thee to his realm. For such protection it is always possible to make provision with small payments at regular intervals. Therefore the provident man delays not in expectation of a large sum becoming available for such a wise purpose.

"Counsel with wise men. Seek the advice of men whose daily work is handling money. Let them save you from such an error as I myself made in entrusting my money to the judgment of Azmur, the brick maker. A small return and a safe one is far more desirable than risk.

"Enjoy life while you are here. Do not overstrain or try to save too much. If one tenth of all you earn is as much as you can comfortably keep, be content to keep this portion. Live otherwise according to your income and let not yourself get afraid to spend. Life is good and life is rich with things worth while and things to enjoy."

His friends thanked him and went away. Some were silent because they had no imagination and could not understand. Some were sarcastic because they thought that one so rich should divide with old friends not so fortunate.

But some had in their eyes a new light. They realized that Algamish had come back each time to the room of the scribes because he was watching a man work his way out of darkness into light. When that man had found the light a place awaited him. No one could fill that place until he had for himself worked out his own understanding, until he was ready for opportunity.

These latter were the ones who, in the following years, frequently revisited Arkad, who received them gladly. He counseled with them and gave them freely of his wisdom as men of broad experience are always glad to do. And he assisted them in so investing their savings that it would bring in a good interest with safety and would neither be lost nor entangled in investments that paid no dividends.

THE TURNING POINT in these men's lives came upon that day when they realized the truth that had come from Algamish to Arkad and from Arkad to them.

A Part of All You Earn is Yours to Keep.

SEVEN REMEDIES FOR A LEAN PURSE

Royal Proclamation

THAT ALL MEN MAY HAVE WEALTH. Heed Ye, Heed Ye, My People, the command of thy King.

Babylon, our beloved city, is the richest in all the world. Of gold it possesses wealth untold.

Because a few of our worthy citizens do know the laws of wealth, they have grown exceedingly rich. Because the many of our citizens do not know the laws of wealth, they remain poor.

Therefore, that all my faithful subjects may learn the laws of wealth and be able to acquire gold, have I commanded the wisdom of the wealthy to be taught to all my people.

Be it known that I, your King, have set aside seven days to be devoted to the study of the laws of wealth. Upon the seventeenth day of the first moon do I command all my loyal subjects to seek the teachers I have appointed in every part of our city, that each and all may share justly in the rich treasures of Babylon.

Heed Ye, Heed Ye, My People, the command of thy King.

SARGON KING OF BABYLON

The Tale of Seven Remedies for a Lean Purse

THE glory of Babylon endures. Down through the ages its reputation comes to us as the richest of cities, its treasures as fabulous.

Yet, it was not always so. The riches of Babylon were the results of the money wisdom of its people. They first had to know how to become wealthy.

When the good king, SARGON, returned to Babylon, after defeating his enemies, the Elamites, he was confronted with a serious situation. The royal Chancellor explained it to the king thus:

"After many years of great prosperity brought to our people because your majesty built the great irrigation canals and the mighty temples to God, now that these works are completed the people seem unable to support themselves.

"The laborers are without employment. The merchants have few customers. The farmers are unable to sell their produce. The people have not enough gold to buy food."

"But where has all the gold gone that we spent for these great improvements?" demanded the King.

"It has found its way, I fear," responded the Chancellor, "'into the possession of a few very rich men of our city. It filtered through the fingers of most of our people as quickly as the goat's milk goes through the strainer. Now that the stream of gold has ceased to flow, most of our people have nothing to show for their earnings."

The King was thoughtful for some time. Then he asked, "Why should so few men be able to acquire all the gold?"

"Because they know how," replied the Chancellor. "One may not condemn a man for succeeding because he knows how. Neither may one with justice take away from a man what he has fairly earned, to give to men of less ability."

"But why," demanded the King, "should not all the people learn how to accumulate gold and therefore become themselves rich and prosperous?"

"Quite possible, your excellency. But who can teach them? Certainly not the priests, because they know naught of money making."

"Who knows best in all our city how to become wealthy, Chancellor?" asked the King.

"Thy question answers itself, your majesty. Who has amassed the greatest wealth in Babylon?"

"Well said, my able Chancellor. It is Arkad. He is the richest man in Babylon. Bring him before me on the morrow."

Upon the following day, as the King had decreed, Arkad appeared before him, straight and sprightly despite his three score years and ten.

"Arkad," spoke the King, 'is it true thou art the richest man in Babylon?"

"So it is reported, your majesty, and no man disputes it."

"How becamest thou so wealthy?"

'By taking advantage of opportunities available to all citizens of our good city."

'Thou hadst nothing to start with?"

"Only a great desire for wealth. Besides this, nothing."

"Arkad," continued the King, "our city is in a very unhappy state because a few may know how to acquire wealth and therefore monopolize it, while the mass of our citizens lack the knowledge of how to keep any part of the gold they receive.

"It is my desire that Babylon be the wealthiest city in the world. Therefore, it must be a city of many wealthy men. Therefore, we must teach all the people how to acquire riches. Tell me, Arkad, is there any secret to acquiring wealth? Can it be taught?"

"It is practical, your majesty. That which one man knows can be taught to others."

The king's eyes glowed, "Arkad, thou speaketh the words I wish to hear. Wilt thou lend thyself to this great cause? Wilt thou teach thy knowledge to a school for teachers, each of whom shall teach others until there are enough trained to teach these truths to every worthy subject in my domain?"

Arkad bowed and said, "I am thy humble servant to command. Whatever of knowledge possess will I gladly give for the betterment of my fellowmen and the glory of my King. Let your good chancellor arrange for me a class of one hundred men and I will teach to them those Seven Remedies which did fatten my purse, than which there was none leaner in all Babylon."

A fortnight later, in compliance with the King's command, the chosen hundred assembled in the great hall of the Temple of Learning, seated upon colorful rugs in a semi circle. Arkad sat beside a small taboret upon which smoked a sacred lamp sending forth a strange and pleasing odor.

"Behold the richest man in Babylon," whispered a student, nudging his neighbor as Arkad arose. "He is but a man even as the rest of us."

"As a dutiful subject of our great King," Arkad began, "I stand before you in his service. Because once I was a poor youth who did greatly desire gold, and because I found knowledge that enabled me to acquire it, he asks that I impart unto you my knowledge.

"I started my fortune in the humblest way. I had no advantage not enjoyed as fully by you and every citizen of Babylon.

'The first storehouse of my treasure was a well-worn purse. I loathed its useless emptiness. I desired that it be round and full, clinking with the sound of gold. Therefore, I sought every remedy for a lean purse. I found seven.

''To you, who are assembled before me, shall I explain the 'Seven Remedies for a Lean Purse' which I do recommend to all men who desire much gold. Each day for seven days will I explain to you one of the Seven Remedies.

"Listen attentively to the knowledge that I will impart. Debate it with me. Discuss it among yourselves. Learn these lessons thoroughly, that ye may also plant in your own purses the seeds of wealth. First must each of you start wisely to build a fortune of his own. Then wilt thou be competent, and only then, to teach these truths to others.

"I shall teach to you in simple ways how to fatten your purses. This is the first step leading to the temple of wealth, and no man may climb who cannot plant his feet firmly upon the first step.

"We shall now consider the First Remedy."

THE FIRST REMEDY - Start thy purse to fattening

Arkad addressed a thoughtful man in the second row. "My good friend, at what craft workest thou?"

"I," replied the man, "am a scribe and carve records upon the clay tablets."

"Even at such labor did I myself earn my first coppers. Therefore, thou hast the same opportunity to build a fortune."

He spoke to a florid faced man, farther back. "Pray tell also what dost thou to earn thy bread."

"I," responded this man, "am a meat butcher. I do buy the goats the farmers raise and kill them and sell the meat to the housewives and the hides to the sandal makers."

"Because thou dost also labor and earn, thou hast every advantage to succeed as I did possess."

In this way did Arkad proceed to find out how each man labored to earn his living. When he had done questioning them he said:

"Now, my students, ye can see that there are many trades at which men may earn coins. Each of the ways of earning is a stream of gold from which the worker doth divert by his labors a portion to his own purse. Therefore into the purse of each of you flows a stream of coins large or small according to his ability. Is it not so?"

Thereupon they agreed that it was so.

"Then", continued Arkad, "if each one of you desireth to build himself a fortune, is it not wise to start by utilizing that source of wealth which he has already established?"

To this they agreed.

Then Arkad turned to a humble man who had declared himself an egg merchant. "If thou select one of thy baskets and put into it each morning ten eggs and take out from it each evening nine eggs, what will eventually happen?"

"It will become in time overflowing."

"Why?"

"Because each day I put it one more egg than I take out."

Arkad turned to the class with a smile.

"Does any man here have a lean purse?"

First they looked amused. Then they laughed. Lastly they waved their purses in jest.

"All right," he continued, "now I shall tell thee the first remedy I learned to cure a lean purse. Do exactly as I have suggested to the egg merchant. For every ten coins thou placest within thy purse take out for use but nine. Thy purse will start to fatten at once and its increasing weight will feel good in thy hand and bring satisfaction to thy soul.

"Deride not what I say because of its simplicity. Truth is always simple. I told thee I would tell how I built my fortune. This was my beginning. I, too, carried a lean purse and cursed it because there was naught within to satisfy my desires. But when I began to take out from my purse but nine parts of ten I put in, it began to fatten. So will thine.

"Now I will tell a strange truth, the reason for which I know not, when I ceased to pay out more than nine tenths of my earnings, I managed to get along just as well. I was not shorter than before. Also, ere long, did coins come to me more easily than before. Surely it is a law of God that unto him who keepeth and spendeth not a certain part of all his earnings, shall gold come more easily. Likewise, him whose purse is empty does gold avoid.

"Which desirest thou the most? Is it the gratification of thy desires of each day, a jewel, a bit of finery, better raiment, more food; things quickly gone and forgotten? Or is it substantial belongings, gold, lands, herds, merchandise, income bringing investments? The coins thou takest from thy purse bring the first. The coins thou leavest within it will bring the latter.

"This, my students, was the first remedy I did discover for my lean purse: 'For each ten coins I put in, to spend but nine'. Debate this amongst yourselves. If any man proves it untrue, tell me upon the morrow when we shall meet again."

THE SECOND REMEDY - Control Thy Expenditures

"Some of your members, my students, have asked me this: 'How can a man keep one tenth of all he earns in his purse when all the coins he earns are not enough for his necessary expenses?" So did Arkad address his students upon the second day.

"Yesterday how many of thee carried lean purses?"

"All of us," answered the class.

"Yet, thou do not all earn the same. Some earn much more than others. Some have much larger families to support. Yet, all purses were equally lean. Now I will tell thee an unusual truth about men and sons of men. It is this: That what each of us calls our necessary expenses will always grow to equal our incomes unless we protest to the contrary.

"Confuse not thy necessary expenses with thy desires. Each of you, together with your good families, has more desires than your earnings can gratify. Therefore, are thy earnings spent to gratify these desires insofar as they will go. Still thou retainest many ungratified desires.

"All men are burdened with more desires than they can gratify. Because of my wealth thinkest thou I may gratify every desire? This a false idea. There are limits to my time. There are limits to my strength. There are limits to the distance I may travel. There are limits to what I may eat. There are limits to the zest with which I may enjoy.

"I say to you that just as weeds grow in a field wherever the farmer leaves space for their roots, even so freely do desires grow in men whenever there is a possibility of their being gratified. Thy desires are a multitude and those that thou mayest gratify are but few.

"Study thoughtfully thy accustomed habits of living. Herein may be most often found certain accepted expenses that may wisely be reduced or eliminated. Let thy motto be one hundred per cent of appreciated value demanded for each coin spent.

"Therefore, engrave upon the clay each thing for which thou desireth to spend. Select those that are necessary and others that are possible through the expenditure of nine-tenths of thy income. Cross out the rest and consider them but a part of that great multitude of desires that must go unsatisfied and regret them not.

"Budget then thy necessary expenses. Touch not the one tenth that is fattening thy purse. Let this be thy great desire that is being fulfilled. Keep working with thy budget, keep adjusting it to help thee. Make it thy first assistant in defending thy fattening purse."

Hereupon one of the students, wearing a robe of red and gold, arose and said, "I am a free man. I believe that it is my right to enjoy the good things of life. Therefore do I rebel against the slavery of a budget which determines just how much I may spend and for what. I feel it would take much pleasure from my life and make me little more than a pack ass to carry a burden."

To him Arkad replied. "Who, my friend, would determine thy budget?"

"I would make it for myself," responded the protesting one.

"In that case were a pack ass to budget his burden would he include therein and rugs and heavy bars of gold? Not so. He would include hay and grain and a bag of water for the desert trail.

"The purpose of a budget is to help thy purse to fatten. It is to assist thee to have thy necessities and, in so far as attainable, thy other desires. It is to enable thee to realize thy most cherished desires by defending them from thy casual wishes. Like a bright light in a dark cave thy budget shows up the leaks from thy purse and enable thee to stop them and control thy expenditures for definite and gratifying purposes."

"This then is the second remedy for a lean purse. Budget thy expenses that thou mayest have coins to pay for thy necessities, to pay for thy enjoyments and to gratify thy worthwhile desires without spending more than nine-tenths of thy earnings."

THE THIRD REMEDY - Make thy gold multiply

"Behold thy lean purse is fattening. Thou hast disciplined thyself to leave therein one-tenth of all thou earneth. Thou hast controlled thy expenditures to protect thy growing treasure. Next, we will consider means to put thy treasure to labor and to increase. Gold in a purse is gratifying to own and satisfieth a miserly soul but earns nothing. The gold we may retain from our earnings is but the start. The earnings it will make shall build our fortunes." So spoke Arkad upon the third day to his class.

"How therefore may we put our gold to work? My first investment was unfortunate, for I lost all. Its tale I will relate later. My first profitable investment was a loan I made to a man named Aggar, a shield maker. Once each year did he buy large shipments of bronze brought from across the sea to use in his trade. Lacking sufficient capital to pay the merchants, he would borrow from those who had extra coins. He was an honorable man. His borrowing he would repay, together with an honorable rental, as he sold his shields.

Each time I loaned to him I loaned back also the rental he had paid to me. Therefore not only did my capital increase, but its earnings likewise increased. Most gratifying was it to have these sums return to my purse.

I tell you, my students, a man's wealth is not in the coins he carries in his purse; it is the income he buildeth, the golden stream that continually floweth into his purse and keepeth it always bulging. That is what every man desireth. That is what thou, each one of thee desireth: an income that continueth to come whether thou work or travel.

"Great income I have acquired. So great that I am called a very rich man. My loans to Aggar were my first training in profitable investment. Gaining wisdom from this experience, I expanded my loans and investments as my capital increased. From a few sources at first, from many sources later, flowed into my purse a golden stream of wealth available for such wise uses as I should decide.

"Behold, from my humble earnings I had begotten a hoard of golden slaves, each laboring and earning more gold. As they labored for me, so their children also labored and their children's children until great was the income from their combined efforts.

"Gold increaseth rapidly when making reasonable earnings as thou wilt see from the following: A farmer, when his first son was born, took ten pieces of silver to a money lender and asked him to keep it on rental for his son until he became twenty years of age. This the money lender did, and agreed the rental shall be one-fourth of its value every four years. The farmer asked, because the sum he had set aside as belonging to his son, that the rental be added to the principal.

When the boy had reached the age of twenty years, the farmer again went to the money lender to inquire about the silver. The money lender explained that because this sum had been increased by compound interest, the original ten pieces of silver had now grown to thirty and one half pieces.

The farmer was well pleased and because the son did not need the coins, he left them with the money lender. When the son became fifty years of age, the father meantime having passed to the other world, the money lender paid the son in settlement one hundred and sixty seven pieces of silver.

"Thus in fifty years had the investment multiplied itself at rental almost seventeen times.

"This then is the third remedy for a lean purse, to put each coin to laboring that it may reproduce its kind even as the flocks of the field and help bring to thee income, a stream of wealth that shall flow constantly into thy purse."

THE FOURTH REMEDY - Guard thy treasures from loss

"Misfortune loves a shining mark. Gold in a man's purse must be guarded with firmness, else it be lost. Thus it is wise that we must first secure small amounts and learn to protect them before God entrusts us with larger." So spoke Arkad upon the fourth day to his class.

"Every owner of gold is tempted by opportunities whereby it would seem that he could make large sums by its investment in most plausible projects. Often friends and relatives are eagerly entering such investment and urge him to follow.

"The first sound principle of investment is security for thy principal. Is it wise to be intrigued by larger earnings when thy principal may be lost? I say not. The penalty of risk is probable loss. Study carefully before parting with thy treasure each assurance, that it may be safely reclaimed. Be not misled by thy own romantic desires to make wealth rapidly.

"Before thou loan it to any man assure thy self of his ability to repay and his reputation for doing so, that thou mayest not unwittingly be making him a present of thy hard earned treasure.

"'Before thou entrust it as an investment in any field acquaint thyself with the dangers which may beset it.

"My own first investment was a tragedy to me at the time. The guarded savings of a year I did entrust to a brick maker, named Azmur, who was traveling over the far seas and in Tyre agreed to buy for me the rare jewels of the Phoenicians. These we would sell upon his return and divide the profits. The Phoenicians were scoundrels and sold him bits of glass. My treasure was lost. Today, my training would show to me at once the folly of entrusting a brick maker to buy jewels.

"Therefore, do I advise thee from the wisdom of my experiences: be not too confident of thy own wisdom in entrusting thy treasures to the possible pitfalls of investments. Better far consult the wisdom of those experienced in handling money for profit. Such advice is freely given for the asking and may readily possess a value equal in gold to the sum thou considerest investing. In truth such is its actual value, if it save thee from loss.

"This then is the fourth remedy for a lean purse, and of great importance if it prevent thy purse from being emptied once it has become well filled. Guard thy treasure from loss by investing only where thy principal is safe, where it may be reclaimed if desirable, and where thou will not fail to collect a fair rental. Consult with wise men. Secure the advice of men experienced in the profitable handling of gold. Let their wisdom protect thy from unsafe investment."

THE FIFTH REMEDY - Make of thy dwelling a profitable investment

"If a man setteth aside nine parts of his earnings upon which to live and enjoy life, and if any part of this nine parts he can turn into a profitable investment without detriment to his well being, then so much faster will his treasures grow." So spake Arkad to his class at their fifth lesson.

"All too many of our men of Babylon do raise their families in unseemly quarters. They do pay to exacting landlords liberal rentals for rooms where their wives have not a spot to raise the blooms that gladden a woman's heart and their children have no place to play their games except in the unclean alleys.

"No man's family can fully enjoy life unless they do have a plot of ground wherein children can play in the clean earth and where the wife may raise not only blossoms but good rich herbs to feed her family.

"To a man's heart it brings gladness to eat the figs from his own trees and the grapes of his own vines. To own his own domicile and to have it a place he is proud to care for, putteth confidence in his heart and greater effort behind all his endeavors. Therefore, do I recommend that every man own the roof that sheltereth him and his.

"Nor is it beyond the ability of any well intentioned man to own his home. Hath not our great king so widely extended the walls of Babylon that within them much land is now unused and may be purchased at sums most reasonable.

"Also I say to you, my students, that the money lenders gladly consider the desires of men who seek homes and lands for their families. Readily may thou borrow to pay the brick maker and the builder for such commendable purposes, if thou can show a reasonable portion of the necessary sum which thou thyself hath provided for the purpose.

"Then when the house be build, thou canst pay the money lender with the same regularity as thou didst pay the landlord. Because each payment will reduce thy indebtedness to the moneylender, a few years will satisfy his loan.

"Then will thy heart be glad because thou wilt own in thy own right a valuable property and thy only cost will be the king's taxes.

"Also wilt thy good wife go more often to the river to wash thy robes, that each time returning she may bring a goatskin of water to pour upon the growing things.

"Thus come many blessings to the man who owneth his own house. And greatly will it reduce his cost of living, making available more of his earnings for pleasures and the gratification of his desires. This then is the Fifth Remedy for a lean purse. Own thy own home."

THE SIXTH REMEDY - Insure a future income

'The life of every man proceedeth from his childhood to his old age. This is the path of life and no man may deviate from it unless God calls him prematurely to the world beyond. Therefore, do I say that it behooves a man to make preparation for a suitable income in the days to come, when he is no longer young and to make preparation for his family should he be no longer with them to comfort and support them. This lesson shall instruct thee in providing a full purse when time has made thee less able to earn." So Arkad addressed his class upon the sixth day.

"The man who became of his understanding of the laws of wealth, acquireth a growing surplus, should give thought to those future days. He should plan certain investments or provisions that may endure safely for many years, yet will be available when the time arrives which he has so wisely anticipated.

"There are diverse ways by which a man may provide with safety for his future. He may provide a hiding place and there bury a secret treasure. Yet, no matter with what skill it be hidden it may nevertheless become the loot of thieves. For this reason I recommend not this plan.

"A man may buy houses or lands for this purpose. If wisely chosen as to their usefulness and value in the future, they are permanent in their value, and their earnings or their sale will provide well for his purpose.

"A man may loan a small sum to the money lender and increase it at regular periods. The rental which the money lender adds to this will largely add to its increase. I do know a sandal maker, named Ansan, who explained to me not long ago that each week for eight years he had deposited with his money lender two pieces of silver. The money lender had but recently given him an accounting over which he greatly rejoiced. The total of his small deposits with their rental at the customary rate of one fourth their due for each four years, had now become a thousand and forty pieces of silver.

"I did gladly encourage him further by demonstrating to him with my knowledge of the numbers that in twelve years more, if he would keep his regular deposits of but two pieces of silver each week, the money lender would then owe him four thousand pieces of silver, a worthy competence for the rest of his life.

"Surely when such a small payment made with regularity doth produce such profitable results no man can afford not to insure a treasure for his old age and the protection of his family, no matter how prosperous his business and his investments may be.

"I would that I might say more about this. In my mind rests a belief that some day wise thinking men will devise a plan to insure men against death whereby many men pay in but a trifling sum regularly, the aggregate making a handsome sum for the family of each member who passeth to the beyond. This do I see as something desirable and which I could highly recommend. But today it is not possible because it must reach beyond the life of any man or any partnership to operate. It must be as stable as the King's throne. Some day do I feel that such a plan shall come to pass and be a great blessing to many men, because even the first small payment will make available a fortune for the family of a member should he pass on.

"But because we live in our own day and not in the days which are to come, must we take advantage of those means and ways of accomplishing our purposes. Therefore, do I recommend to all men, that they, by wise and well thought out methods, do provide against a lean purse in their mature years. For a lean purse to a man no longer able to earn or to a family without its head is a sore tragedy.

"This then is the Sixth Remedy for a lean Purse. Provide in advance for the needs of thy growing age and the protection of thy family."

THE SEVENTH REMEDY - Increase thy ability to earn

'This day do I speak to thee, my students, of one of the most vital remedies for a lean purse. Yet, I will talk not of gold but of yourselves, of the men beneath the robes of many colors who do sit before me. I will talk to you of those things within the minds and lives of men which do work for or against their success." So did Arkad address his class upon the seventh day.

"Not long ago came to me a young man seeking to borrow. When I questioned him the cause of his necessity, he complained that his earnings were insufficient to pay his expenses. Thereupon I explained to him, this being the case, he was a poor customer for the money lender, as he possessed no surplus earning capacity to repay the loan.

"'What you need, young man', I told him, 'is to earn more coins. What dost thou to increase thy capacity to earn?

"'All that I can do', he replied. 'Six times within two moons have I approached my master to request my pay be increased, but without success. No man can go oftener than that.'

"We may smile at his simplicity, yet he did possess one of the vital requirements to increase his earnings. Within him was a strong desire to earn more, a proper and commendable desire.

"Preceding accomplishment must be desire. Thy desires must be strong and definite. General desires are but weak longings. For a man to wish to be rich is of little purpose. For a man to desire five pieces of gold is a tangible desire which he can press to fulfillment. After he has backed his desire for five pieces of gold with strength of purpose to secure it, next he can find similar ways to obtain ten pieces and then twenty pieces and later a thousand pieces and behold, he has become wealthy. In learning to secure his one definite small desire he hath trained himself to secure a larger one. This is the process by which wealth is accumulated; first in small sums, then in larger ones as a man learns and becomes more capable.

"Desires must be simple and definite. They defeat their own purpose should they be too many, too confusing, or beyond the training to accomplish.

"As a man perfecteth himself in his calling even so doth is ability to earn increase. In those days when I was a humble scribe carving upon the clay for a few coppers each day, I observed that other workers did more than I and were paid more. Therefore, did I determine that I would be exceeded by none. Nor did it take long for me to discover the reason for their greater success. More interest in my work, more concentration upon my task, more persistence in my effort, and behold, few men could carve more tablets in a day than I. With reasonable promptness my increased skill was rewarded, nor was it necessary for me to go six times to my master to request recognition.

'The more of wisdom we know, the more we may earn. That man who seeks to learn more of his craft shall be richly rewarded. If he is an artisan, he may seek to learn the methods and the tools of those most skillful in the same line. If he laboreth at the law or at healing, he may consult and exchange knowledge with others of his calling. If he be a merchant, he may continually seek better goods that can be purchased at lower prices.

"Always do the affairs of man change and improve because keen minded men seek greater skill that they may better serve those upon whose patronage they depend. Therefore, I urge all men to be in the front rank of progress and not to stand still, lest they be left behind.

"Many things come to make a man's life rich with gainful experiences. Such things as following, a man must do if he shall respect himself:

"He must pay his debts with all promptness within his power, not purchasing that for which he is unable to pay.

"He must take care of his family that they may think and speak well of him.

"He must make a will of record that in case God calls him, proper and honorable division of his property be accomplished.

"He must have compassion upon those who are injured or smitten by misfortune and aid them within reasonable limits. He must do deeds of thoughtfulness to those dear to him.

"Thus the seventh and last remedy for a lean purse is to cultivate thy own powers, to study and become wiser, to become more skillful, to so act as to respect thyself. Thereby shalt thou acquire confidence in thyself to achieve thy carefully considered desires.

'These then are the Seven Remedies for a Lean Purse, which, out of the experience of a long and successful life I do urge for all men who desire wealth.

"There is MORE GOLD in BABYLON, my students, than thou dreamest of. There is abundance for all.

"Go thou forth and practice these truths that thou mayest prosper and grow wealthy, as is thy right.

"Go thou forth and teach these truths that every honorable subject of his majesty may also share liberally in the ample wealth of our beloved city. THIS IS THY KING'S COMMAND!"

The Debate of Good Luck

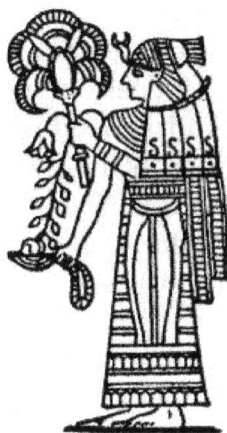

THE Temple of Learning in old Babylon was an unusual institution. In this spacious building many groups of men would congregate each evening about their favorite leaders to discuss interesting subjects.

Within the doors of this temple all men met as equals. Here the humblest slave could discuss upon an equal footing with a prince of the royal house.

When Arkad arrived at his special corner upon a certain evening, four score men reclining upon the small rugs were awaiting him.

"What shall we discuss this night?" inquired Arkad.

"I have a subject," ventured a tall cloth weaver, arising as was the custom. "'This day I am lucky, for I have found a purse in which are pieces of gold. To continue to be lucky is my great desire. Feeling that all men share with me this desire, I do suggest we debate good luck. Let us seek to discover if there be ways it can be enticed to one."

"A most interesting subject has been offered to us," Arkad resumed. 'To some, good luck bespeaks but a chance happening that may come to any man. Others do believe that the instigator of all good fortune is 'good luck', which is attracted to a favored few. What say you, my friends, shall we seek to find if there be means by which good luck may be enticed to visit each and all of us?"

"Yea! Yea! And much of it!" responded his listeners.

"To seek good luck requireth action upon our part. Who among you will offer a suggestion as to where we shall begin our search?" queried Arkad.

"That I will do," spoke a well-robed youth, arising. "When a man speaketh of luck is it not natural that his thoughts should turn to the gaming tables? Is it not there where we may find many men courting good luck in the hope that it will favor them with rich winnings?"

"Continue thy story," called a voice as he resumed his seat. "Didst thou find good luck there?"

"I am not averse to admitting it seemed not to know that I was there," he replied

"How about you? Have you found it awaiting you in such places?"

"A wise start," broke in Arkad. "We meet here to consider all sides of each question. To ignore the gaming tables would be to pass by an instinct quite common in most men, the love of taking a chance with the hope of winning."

"That doth remind me of the races yesterday", called another man. "If luck frequents the gaming tables, certainly it does not overlook the races, which, to me, are far more pleasure. Tell us, Arkad, didst good luck whisper to you to bet upon those greys from Nineveh? I did stand right behind when thou placeth thy bet and could scarce believe my ears, good as they are. You know as well as all of us that no team can beat our beloved bays. Does it not look as though good luck whispered in his ear that the inside black was to stumble as they made the last turn and trip the bays to give the greys an unearned victory?"

Arkad smiled good humoredly at the banter. "What reasons have we to think that luck would take that much interest in any man's bet upon a horse race? I find it not at the gaming tables either, where men lose more gold they can win.

"In honest trading as in buying and selling, a man may expect to make a profit upon his transactions. Perhaps not upon all because sometimes he may act without good judgment.

But if he persists he may usually expect to make his profit. This is so because the chance of profit is always in his favor.

"But when a man playeth the games the chance of profit is always against him and always in favor of the game keeper. The game is so arranged to favor the keeper. It is his business at which he plans to make a liberal profit for himself. Few men realize how certain the game keeper's profit and how poor their own chance to win.

"Thus for an example it will be well for us to consider wagering upon the cube. Each time it is cast we bet which side will be uppermost. If it be the red side the game master pays to us four times our bet. If it shows any one of the other five sides uppermost, we lose. Thus the figures show that for each cast the player has five chances to lose and because the red pays four to one, he has four chances to win. In a night's play the game master expects to keep for his own one fifth of all the wagers made. Can any man expect to win consistently against such odds so arranged that he should lose consistently?"

"Yet some men do win large sums at times," volunteered one of the listeners.

"Quite so, they do," Arked continued. "Realizing this, the thought has often come to me whether money secured in such ways brings any worth while value to those who receive it. Among my acquaintances are many of the successful men of Babylon, yet among them I can not name one who can trace his start to such a source. You who are here tonight must know a great many more of the substantial citizens of our city. To me it would be of interest to learn how many of our better citizens can credit the gaming tables with their start or their support. What say you?"

There was a prolonged pause. Finally a voice enquired, "Wouldst thy enquiry include the game keeper?"

"If not one of you can think of anyone else. But wait, how about yourselves? Are there any consistent winners with us here who hesitate to advise us about the sources of their incomes?"

His challenge was answered by a loud groan from the rear taken up and spread by others amid much laughter. "It would look that we were seeking far from where we should.

"Who among you has at any time had good luck such as our friend, the cloth weaver, finding gold or valuables? What, no one? Then, rare indeed be this kind of good luck. Who among you have had good luck within thy reach only to let it escape?"

Many hands were raised. "Speak up one of you! Let us hear how it could escape you. Who shall be the first?"

An elderly merchant arose, smoothing his genteel white robes. "With thy permission, most honorable Arkad, and friends, I will gladly relate a tale that doth illustrate how closely unto a man good luck may approach and how blindly he may permit it to escape, much to his loss.

"Many years ago when a young man, just married and well started to earning, my father did come one day and urge most strongly that I enter upon an investment. The son of one of his good friends had taken notice of a barren tract of land not far beyond the outer walls of our city. It lay high above the canal where no water could reach it.

"The son of my father's friend devised a plan to purchase this land, build three large water wheels that could be operated by oxen and thereby raise the life giving waters to the fertile soil. This accomplished, he planned to divide into small tracts and sell to the residents of the city for herb patches.

"The son of my father's friend did not possess sufficient gold to complete such an undertaking. Like myself, he was a young man earning a fair sum. His father, like mine, was a man of large family and small means. He, therefore, decided to interest a group of men to enter the enterprise with him. The group was to comprise twelve, each of whom must be a money earner and agree to pay one tenth of his earnings into the enterprise until the land was made ready for sale. All would then share justly in the profits in proportion to their investment.

"'Thou, my son', bespoke my father to me, 'art now in thy young manhood. It is deep desire that thou begin the building valuable estate for thyself that thou mayest become respected among men. I desire to see thou profit from a knowledge of the thoughtless mistakes of thy father'.

"This do I most ardently desire, my father," I replied.

"'Then, this do I advise. Do what I should have done at thy age. From thy earnings keep out one tenth to put into favorable investments. With this one tenth of thy earnings and what it will also earn, thou canst, before thou art my age, accumulate for thyself a valuable estate'.

"Thy words are words of wisdom, my father. Greatly do I desire riches. Yet there are many uses to which my earnings are called. Therefore, do I hesitate to do as thou dost advise. I am young. There is plenty of time'.

"'So, I thought at thy age, yet behold, many years have passed and I have not yet made the beginning'.

"We live in a different age, my father, I shall avoid thy mistakes".

"'Opportunity stands before thee, my son. It is offering a chance that may lead to wealth. I beg of thee do not delay. Go upon the morrow to the son of my friend and bargain with him to pay ten percent of thy earnings into this investment. Go promptly upon the morrow. Opportunity waits for no man. Today it is here; soon it is gone. Therefore, delay not!'

"In spite of the advice of my father, I did hesitate. There were beautiful new robes just brought by the tradesmen from the East, robes of such richness and beauty, my good wife and I felt we must each possess one. Should I agree to pay one tenth of my earnings into the enterprise, we must deprive ourselves of these and other pleasures we dearly desired. I delayed making a decision until it was too late, much to my subsequent regret. The enterprise did prove to be more profitable than any man had prophesied. This is my tale, showing how I did permit good luck to escape."

"In this tale we see how good luck waits to come to that man who accepts opportunity," commented a swarthy man of the desert. "To the building of an estate there must always be the beginning. That start may be a few pieces of gold or silver which a man diverts from his earnings to his first investment. I, myself, am the owner of many herds. The start of my herds I did begin when I was a mere boy and did purchase with one piece of silver a young calf. This, being the beginning of my wealth was of great importance to me.

'To take his first start to building an estate is as good luck as can come to any man. With all men, that first step, which changes them from men who earn from their own labor to men who draw dividends from the earnings of their gold, is important. Some, fortunately, take it when young and thereby outstrip in financial success those who do take it later or those unfortunate men like the father of this merchant who never take it.

"Had our friend, the merchant, taken this step in his early manhood when this opportunity came to him, this day he would be blessed with much more of this world's goods. Should the good luck of our friend, the cloth weaver, cause him to take such a step at this time, it will indeed be but the beginning of much greater good fortune."

"'Thank you! I like to speak, also." A stranger from another country arose. "I am a Syrian. Not so well do I speak your tongue. I wish to call this friend, the merchant, a name. Maybe you think it not polite, this name. Yet I wish to call him that. But, alas, I not know your word for it. If I do call it in Syrian, you will not understand. Therefore, please some good gentlemen, tell me that right name you call man who puts off doing those things that mighty good for him."

"Procrastinator," called a voice.

'That's him," shouted the Syrian, waving his hands excitedly, "he accepts not opportunity when she comes. He waits. He says I have much business right now. Bye and bye I talk to you. Opportunity, she will not wait for such slow fellow. She thinks if a man desires to be lucky he will step quick. Any man who not step quick when opportunity comes, he big procrastinator like our friend, this merchant."

The merchant arose and bowed good naturedly in response to the laughter. "My admiration stranger within our gates, who hesitates not to speak the truth."

"And now let us hear another tale of opportunity. Who has for us another experience?" demanded Arkad.

"I have," responded a red robed man of middle age. "I am a buyer of animals, mostly camels and horses. Sometimes I do also buy the sheep and goats. The tale I am about to relate will tell truthfully how opportunity came one night when I did least expect it. Perhaps for this reason I did let it escape. Of this you shall be the judge.

"Returning to the city one evening after a disheartening ten days journey in search of camels, I was much angered to find the gates of the city closed and locked. While my slaves spread our tent for the night, which we must spend with little food and no water, I was approached by an elderly farmer who, like ourselves, found himself locked outside.

'Honored sir', he addressed me, 'from thy appearance I do judge thee to be a buyer. If this be so, much would I like to sell to thee the most excellent flock of sheep just driven up. Alas, my good wife lies very sick with the fever. I must return with all haste. Buy thou my sheep that I and my slaves may mount our camels and travel back without delay'.

"So dark it was that I could not see his flock, but from the bleating I did know it must be large. Having wasted ten days searching for camels I could not find, I was glad to bargain with him. In his anxiety, he did set a most reasonable price. I accepted, well knowing my slaves could drive the flock through the city gates in the morning and sell at a substantial profit.

"The bargain concluded, I called my slaves to bring torches that we might count the flock which the farmer declared to contain nine hundred. I shall not burden you, my friends, with a description of our difficulty in attempting to count so many thirsty, restless, milling sheep. It proved to be an impossible task. Therefore, I bluntly informed the farmer I would count them at daylight and pay him then.

'Please, most honorable sir', he pleaded. 'Pay me but two thirds of the price tonight that I may be on my way. I will leave my most intelligent and educated slave to assist to make the count in the morning. He is trustworthy and to him thou canst pay the balance'.

"But I was stubborn and refused to make payment that night. Next morning, before I awoke, the city gates opened and four buyers rushed out in search of flocks. They were most eager and willing to pay high prices because the city was threatened with siege, and food was not plentiful. Nearly three times the price at which he had offered the flock to me, did the old farmer receive for it. Thus was rare good luck allowed to escape."

"Here is a tale most unusual," commented Arkad. "What wisdom doth it suggest?"

"The wisdom of making a payment immediately when we are convinced our bargain is wise," suggested a venerable saddle maker. "If the bargain be good, then dost thou need protection against thy own weaknesses as much as against any other man. We mortals are changeable. Alas, I must say more apt to change our minds when right than wrong. Wrong, we are stubborn indeed. Right, we are prone to vacillate and let opportunity escape. My first judgment is my best. Yet always have I found it difficult to compel myself to proceed with a good bargain when made. Therefore, as a protection against my own weaknesses, I do make a prompt deposit thereon. This doth save me from later regrets for the good luck that should have been mine."

"Thank you! Again I like to speak." The Syrian was upon his feet once more. 'These tales much alike. Each time opportunity fly away for same reason. Each time she come to procrastinator, bringing good plan. Each time they hesitate, not say, right now best time, I do it quick. How can men succeed that way?"

"Wise are thy words, my friend," responded the buyer. "Good luck fled from procrastination in both these tales. Yet, this is not unusual. The spirit of procrastination is within all men. We desire riches; yet, how often when opportunity doth appear before us, that spirit of procrastination from within doth urge various delays in our acceptance. In listening to it we do become our own worst enemies.

"In my younger days I did not know it by this long word our friend from Syria doth enjoy. I did think at first it was my own poor judgment that did cause me loss of many profitable trades. Later, I did credit it to my stubborn disposition. At last, I did recognize it for what it was – a habit of needless delaying where action was required, action prompt and decisive. How I did hate it when its true character stood revealed. With the bitterness of a wild ass hitched to a chariot, I did break loose from this enemy to my success."

'Thank you! I like ask question from Mr. Merchant." The Syrian was speaking. "You wear fine robes, not like those of poor man. You speak like successful man. Tell us, do you listen now when procrastination whispers in your ear?"

"Like our friend the buyer, I also had to recognize and conquer procrastination," responded the merchant. "To me, it proved to be an enemy, ever watching and waiting to thwart my accomplishments. The tale I did relate is but one of many similar instances I could tell to show how it drove away my opportunities. 'Tis not difficult to conquer, once understood. No man willingly permits the thief to rob his him of grain. Nor does any man willingly permit an enemy to drive away his customers and rob him of his profits. When once I did recognize that such acts as these my enemy was committing, with determination I conquered it. So must every man master his own spirit of procrastination before he can expect to share in the rich treasures of Babylon.

"What sayest, Arkad? Because thou art the richest man in Babylon, many do proclaim thee to be the luckiest. Dost agree with me that no man can arrive at a full measure of success until he hath completely crushed the spirit of procrastination within him?

"It is even as thou sayest," Arkad admitted. "During my long life I have watched generation following generation, marching forward along those avenues of trade, science and learning that lead to success in life. Opportunities came to all these men. Some grasped theirs and moved steadily to the gratification of their deepest desires, but the majority hesitated, faltered and fell behind."

Arkad turned to the cloth weaver. 'Thou didst suggest that we debate good luck. Let us hear what thou now thinkest upon the subject."

"I do see good luck in a different light. I had thought of it as something most desirable that might happen to a man without effort upon his part. Now, I do realize such happenings are not the sort of thing one may attract to him self. From our discussion have I learned that to attract good luck to oneself, it is necessary to take advantage of opportunities. Therefore, in the future I shall endeavor to make the best of such opportunities as do come to me."

''Thou hast well grasped the truths brought forth in our discussion," Arkad replied. "Good luck, we do find, often follows opportunity but seldom comes otherwise. Our merchant friend would have found great good luck had he accepted the opportunity the good goddess did present to him. Our friend the buyer, likewise, would have enjoyed good luck had he completed the purchase of the flock and sold at such a handsome profit.

"We did pursue this discussion to find a means by which good luck could be enticed to us. I feel that we have found the way. Both the tales did illustrate how good luck follows opportunity. Herein lies a truth that many similar tales of good luck, won or lost, could not change. The truth is this: Good luck can be enticed by accepting opportunity.

'Those eager to grasp opportunities for their betterment, do attract 'good luck'. It seems to favor men of action best. Therefore, if a plan be for thy best interest, promptly accept it. If it be against thy best interest, with equal promptness, reject it.

"ACTION will lead thee forward to the successes thou dost desire".
Men of Action are favored by Good Luck

The Tale of The Five Laws of Gold

"A BAG heavy with gold or a clay tablet carved with words of wisdom: if thou hadst thy choice, which wouldst thou choose?"

By the flickering light from the fire of desert shrubs, the sun tanned faces of his listeners gleamed with interest.

"The GOLD, the GOLD," chorused the twenty seven.

Old Kalabab smiled knowingly.

"Hark," he resumed, raising his hand. "Hear the wild dogs out there in the night. They howl and wail because they are lean with hunger. Yet feed them, and what do they? Fight and strut. Then fight and strut some more, giving no thought to the morrow that will surely come.

"Just so it is with the sons of men. Give them a choice of gold and wisdom – what do they do? Ignore the wisdom and waste the gold. On the morrow they wail because they have no more gold.

"Gold is reserved for those who know its laws and abide by them."

Kalabab drew his white robe close about his lean legs, for a cool night wind was blowing.

"Because thou hast served me faithfully upon our long journey, because thou cared well for my camels, because thou toiled uncomplainingly across the hot sands of the desert, because thou fought bravely the robbers that sought to despoil my merchandise, I will tell thee this night the tale of the 'FIVE LAWS OF GOLD', such a tale as thou never hast heard before."

"Hark ye, with deep attention to the words I speak, for if you grasp their meaning and heed them, in the days that come thou shalt have much gold."

He paused impressively. Above in a canopy of blue, the stars shone brightly in the crystal clear skies of Babylonia. Behind the group loomed their faded tents tightly staked against possible desert storms. Beside the tents were neatly stacked bales of merchandise covered with skins. Nearby the camel herd sprawled in the sand, some chewing their cuds contentedly, others snoring in hoarse discord.

"Thou hast told us many good tales, Kalabab" spoke up the chief packer "We look to thy wisdom to guide us upon the morrow when our service with thee shall be at an end."

"I have but told thee of my adventures in strange and distant lands, but this night I shall tell thee of the wisdom of Arkad, the wise rich man."

"Much have we heard of him," edged the chief packer, "for he was the richest man that ever lived in Babylon."

"The richest man he was, and that because he was wise in the ways of gold, even as no man had ever been before him. This night shall I tell of his great wisdom as it was told to me by Nomasir his son, many years ago in Nineveh, when I was but a lad.

"My master and myself had tarried long into the night in the palace of Nomasir. I had helped my master bring great bundles of fine rugs, each one to be tried by Nomasir until his choice of colors was satisfied. At last he was well pleased and commanded us to sit with him and to drink a rare vintage odorous to the nostrils and most warming to my stomach, which was unaccustomed to such a drink. Then, did he tell us this tale of the great wisdom of Arkad, his father, even as I shall tell it to you.

"In Babylon it is the custom, as you know, that the sons of wealthy fathers live with their parents in expectation of inheriting the estate. Arkad did not approve of this custom. Therefore, when young Nomasir reached the man's estate, he sent for the young man and addressed him:

"'My son, it is my desire that thou succeed to my estate. Thou must, however, first prove that thou art capable of wisely handling it. Therefore, I wish that thou go out into the world and show thy ability both to acquire gold, and to make thyself respected among men.

"'To start thee well, I will give thee two things of which I, myself, was denied when I started as a poor youth to build up a fortune.

"'First, I give thee this bag of gold. If thou use it wisely, it will be the basis of thy future success.

"'Second, I give thee this clay tablet upon which are carved "THE FIVE LAWS OF GOLD." If thou dost but interpret them in thy own acts, they shall bring thee competence and security.

"'Ten years from this day come thou back to the house of thy father and give account of thyself. If thou prove worthy, I will then make thee the heir to my estate. Otherwise, I will give it to the priests that they barter for my soul the kind consideration God.

"So Nomasir went forth to make his own way, taking his bag of gold, the clay tablet carefully wrapped in silken cloth, his slave and the horses upon which they rode.

"The ten years passed, and Nomasir, as he had agreed, returned to the house of his father who provided a great feast in his honor, to which he invited many friends and relatives. After the feast was over, the father and mother mounted their throne like seats at one side of the great hall, and Nomasir stood before them to give an account of himself as he had promised his father.

"It was evening. The room was hazy with smoke from the wicks of the oil lamps that but dimly lighted it. Slaves in white woven jackets and tunics fanned the humid air rhythmically with long stemmed palm leaves. A stately dignity colored the scene. The wife of Nomasir and his two young sons, with friends and other members of the family, sat upon rugs behind him, eager listeners.

"'My father,' he began deferentially, "'I bow before thy wisdom. Ten years ago when I stood at the gates of manhood, thou bade me go forth and become a man among men, instead of remaining a vassal to thy fortune.

"'Thou gave me liberally of thy gold. Thou gave me liberally of thy wisdom. Of the gold, alas! I must admit of a disastrous handling It fled, indeed, from my inexperienced hands even as a wild hare flees at the first opportunity from the youth who captures it.

The father smiled indulgently. 'Continue, my son, thy tale interests me in all its details.'

"'I decided to go to Nineveh, as it was a growing city, believing that I might find there opportunities. I joined a caravan and among its members made numerous friends. Two well spoken men who had a most beautiful white horse as fleet as the wind, were among these.

"'As we journeyed, they told me in confidence that in Nineveh was a wealthy man who owned a horse so swift that it had never been beaten. Its owner believed that no horse living could run with greater speed. Therefore, would he wager any sum however large that his horse could out speed any horse in all Babylonia. Compared to their horse, so my friends said, it was but a lumbering ass that could be beaten with ease.

"'They offered, as a great favor, to permit me to join them in a wager. I was quite carried away with the plan.

"'Our horse was badly beaten and I lost much of my gold.' The father laughed. "Later, I discovered that this was a deceitful plan of these men and they constantly journeyed with caravans seeking victims. You see, the man in Nineveh was their partner and shared with them the bets he won. This shrewd deceit taught me my first lesson in looking out for myself.

"'I was soon to learn another, equally bitter. In the caravan was another young man with whom I became quite friendly. He was the son of wealthy parents and like myself, journeying to Nineveh to find a suitable location. Not long after our arrival, he told me that a merchant had died and his shop with its rich merchandise and patronage could be secured at a paltry price. Saying that we would be equal partners, but first he must return to Babylon to secure his gold, he prevailed upon me to purchase the stock with my gold, agreeing that his would be used later to carry on our venture.

"'He long delayed the trip to Babylon, proving in the meantime to be an unwise buyer and a foolish spender. I finally put him out, but not before the business had deteriorated to where we had only unsaleable goods and no gold to buy other goods. I sacrificed what was left to an Israelite for a pitiful sum.

"'Soon there followed, I tell you, my father, bitter days. I sought employment and found it not, for I was without trade or training that would enable me to earn. I sold my horses. I sold my slave. I sold my extra robes that I might have food and a place to sleep, but each day grim want crouched closer.

"'But in those bitter days, I remembered thy confidence in me, my father. Thou hadst sent me forth to become a man, and this I was determined to accomplish.' The mother buried her face and wept softly.

"'At this time, I bethought me of the tablet thou had given to me upon which thou had carved "THE FIVE LAWS OF GOLD." Thereupon, I read most carefully thy words of wisdom, and realized that had I but sought wisdom first, my gold would not have been lost to me. I learned by heart each law, determined that when once more the goddess of good fortune smiled upon me, I would be guided by the wisdom of age and not by the inexperience of youth.

"'For the benefit of you who are seated here this night, I will read the wisdom of my father as engraved upon the clay tablet which he gave to me ten years ago.'

THE FIVE LAWS OF GOLD

I. Gold cometh gladly and in increasing quantity to any man whosoever will put by not less than one-tenth of his earnings to create an estate for his future and that of his family.

II. Gold laboreth diligently and contentedly for the wise owner who finds for it profitable employment, multiplying even as the flocks of the field.

III. Gold clingeth to the protection of the cautious owner who invests it under the advice of men wise in its handling.

IV. Gold slippeth away from the man who invests it in businesses or purposes with which he is not familiar or which are not approved by those skilled in its keep.

V. Gold flees the man who would force it to impossible earnings or who followeth the alluring advice of tricksters and schemers or who trusts it to his own inexperience and romantic desires in investment.

"'These are the five laws of gold as written by my father. I do proclaim them as of greater value than gold itself, as I will show by the continuance of my tale."

"He again faced his father. 'I have told thee of the depth of poverty and despair to which my experience brought me.

"'However there is no chain of disasters that will not come to an end. Mine came when I secured employment managing a crew of slaves working upon the new outer wall of the city.

"'Profiting from my knowledge of the first law of gold, I saved a copper from my first earnings, adding to it at every opportunity until I had a piece of silver. It was a slow procedure, for one must live. I did spend grudgingly, I admit, because I was determined to earn back before the ten years were over, as much gold as you, my Father, had given to me.

"'One day the slave master with whom I had become quite friendly, said to me: "Thou art a thrifty youth who spends not wantonly what he earns. Hast thou gold put by that is not earning?"

"'Yes", I replied, "it is my greatest desire to accumulate gold to replace that which my father gave to me and which I have lost."

"'Tis a worthy ambition, I will grant, and do you know that the gold which you have saved can work for you and earn much more gold?"

"'Alas! My experience has been bitter, for my father's gold has fled me, and I am in much fear lest mine own do the same".

"'If thou hast confidence in me, I will give thee a lesson in the profitable handling of gold," he replied. "Within a year the outer wall will be complete and ready for the great gates of bronze that will be built at each entrance to protect the city from the king's enemies. In all Nineveh there is not enough metal to make these gates and the king has not thought to provide it. Here is my plan: A group of us will pool our gold and send a caravan to the mines of copper and tin, which are distant, and bring to Nineveh the metal for the gates. When the king says, 'Make the great gates', we alone can supply the metal and a rich price he will pay. If the king will not buy from us, we will yet have the metal which can be sold for a fair price."

"'In his offer I recognized an opportunity to abide by the third law and invest my savings under the guidance of wise men. Nor was I disappointed. Our pool was a success, and my small store of gold was greatly increased by the transaction.

"'In due time, I was accepted as a member of this same group in other ventures. They were men wise in the profitable handling of gold. They talked over each plan presented with great care, before entering upon it. They would take no chance on losing their principal or tying it up in unprofitable investments from which their gold could not be recovered. Such foolish things as the horse race and the partnership into which I had entered with my inexperience, would have had scant consideration with them. They would have immediately pointed out their weaknesses.

"'Through my association with these men, I learned to safely invest gold to bring profitable returns. As the years went on, my treasure increased more and more rapidly. I not only made back as much as I lost, but much more.

"'Through my misfortunes, my trials and my success, I have tested time and again the wisdom of the Five Laws of Gold, my father, and have proven them true in every test. To him who is without knowledge of the Five Laws, Gold comes not often, and goeth away quickly. But to him who abideth by the Five Laws, Gold comes and works as his dutiful Slave.'"

Nomasir ceased speaking and motioned to a slave in the back of the room. The slave brought forward, one at a time, three heavy leather bags. One of these Nomasir took and placed upon the floor before his father addressing him again:

"Thou did give to me a bag of gold, Babylon gold. Behold in its place, I do return to thee a bag of Nineveh gold of equal weight. An equal exchange as all will agree.

"Thou didst give to me a clay tablet inscribed with wisdom. Behold, in its stead, I do return two bags of gold." So saying, he took from the slave the other two bags and, likewise, placed them upon the floor before his father.

"This I do to prove to thee, my father, of how much greater value I consider thy wisdom than thy gold. Yet, who can measure in bags of gold, the value of wisdom? Without wisdom, gold is quickly lost by those who have it, but with wisdom, gold can be secured by those who have it not, as these three bags of gold do prove.

"It does, indeed, give to me the deepest satisfaction, my father, to stand before thee and say that, because of thy wisdom, I have been able to become rich and respected before men."

The father placed his hand fondly upon the head of Nomasir. "Thou hast learned well thy lessons, and I am, indeed, fortunate to have a son to whom I may entrust my wealth."

Kalabab ceased his tale and looked critically at his listeners.

"What means this to thee, this tale of Nomasir?" he continued.

"Who amongst thee can go to thy father or to the father of thy wife and give an account of wise handling of his earnings?"

"What would these venerable men think were you to say, 'I have traveled much and learned much and labored much and earned much, yet alas, of gold I have little. Some I spent wisely, and some I spent foolishly and much I lost in unwise ways'.

"Dost still think if but an inconsistency of fate that some men have much gold and others have naught? Then you err.

"Men have much gold when they know the Five Laws of Gold and abide thereby.

"Because I learned these Five Laws in my youth and abided by them, I have become a wealthy merchant. Not by some strange magic did I accumulate my wealth.

"Wealth that comes quickly goeth the same way.

"Wealth that stayeth to give enjoyment and satisfaction to its owner, comes gradually, because it is a child born of knowledge and persistent purpose.

"To earn wealth is but a slight burden upon the thoughtful man. Bearing the burden consistently from year to year accomplishes the final purpose.

"The Five Laws of Gold offer to thee a rich reward for their observance.

"Each of these Five Laws is rich with meaning and lest thou overlook this in the briefness of my tale, I will now repeat them. I do know them each by heart because in my youth, I could see their value and would not be content until I knew them word for word."

The First Law

Gold cometh gladly and in increasing quantity to any man whosoever will put by not less than one-tenth of his earnings to create an estate for his future and that of his family.

"Any man who will put by one-tenth of his earnings consistently and invest it wisely, will surely create a valuable estate that will provide an income for him in the future and further guarantee safety for his family in case God calls him to the world of darkness. This law also sayeth that gold cometh gladly to such a man. I can truly certify this in my own life. The more gold I accumulate, the more readily it comes to me and in increased quantities. The gold which I save earns more, even as yours will, and its earnings earn more, and this is the working out of the first law."

The Second Law

Gold laboreth diligently and contentedly for the wise owner who finds for it profitable employment, multiplying even as the flocks of the field.

"Gold, indeed, is a willing worker. It is ever eager to multiply when opportunity presents itself. To every man who hath a store of gold set by, opportunity comes for its most profitable use. As the years pass, it multiplies itself in surprising fashion."

The Third Law

Gold clingeth to the protection of the cautious owner who invests it under the advice of men wise in its handling.

"Gold, indeed, clingeth to the cautious owner, even as it flees the careless owner. The man who seeks the advice of men wise in handling gold, soon learneth not to jeopardize his treasure, but to preserve in safety and to enjoy in contentment its consistent increase."

The Fourth Law of Gold

Gold slippeth sway from the man who invests it in businesses or purposes with which he not familiar or which are not approved by those skilled in its keep.

"To the man who hath gold, yet is not skilled in its handling, many uses for it appear most profitable. Too often these are fraught with danger of loss, and if properly analyzed by wise men, show small possibility of profit. Therefore, the inexperienced owner of gold who trusts to his own judgment and invests it in business or purposes with which he is not familiar, too often finds his judgment imperfect, and pays with his treasure for his inexperience. Wise indeed, is he who investeth his treasures under the advice of men skilled in the ways of gold."

The Fifth Law of Gold

Gold flees the man who would force it to impossible earnings or who followeth the alluring advice of tricksters and schemers or who trusts it to his own inexperience and romantic desires in its investment.

"Fanciful propositions that thrill like adventure tales always come to the new owner of gold. These appear to endow his treasure with magic powers that will enable it to make impossible earnings. Yet heed ye the wise men for verily they know the risks that lurk behind every plan to make great wealth suddenly.

"Forget not the rich men of Nineveh who would take no chance of losing their principal or tying it up in unprofitable investments.

"This ends my tale of 'The Five Laws of Gold.' In telling it to thee, I have told the secrets of my own success.

"'Yet, they are not secrets but truths which every man must first learn and then follow who wishes to step out of the multitude that, like yon wild dogs, must worry each day for food to eat.

"Tomorrow, we enter Babylon. Look! See the fire that burns eternal above the Temple of Bel! We are already in sight of the golden city. Tomorrow, each of thee shall have gold, the gold thou hast so well earned by thy faithful services.

"Ten years from this night, what can you tell about this gold?

"If there be men among you, who, like Nomasir, will use a portion of their gold to start for themselves an estate and be thenceforth wisely guided by the wisdom of Arkad, ten years from now, 'tis a safe wager, like the son of Arkad, they will be rich and respected among men.

"Our wise acts accompany us through life to please us and to help us. Just as surely, our unwise acts follow us to plague and torment us. Alas, they cannot be forgotten. In the front rank of the torments that do follow us, are the memories of the things we should have done, of the opportunities which came to us and we took not.

"Rich are the Treasures of Babylon, so rich no man can count their value in pieces of gold. Each year, they grow richer and more valuable. Like the treasures of every land, they are a reward, a rich reward awaiting those men of purpose who determine to secure their just share.

"In the strength of thine own desires is a magic power. Guide this power with thy knowledge of 'The Five Laws of Gold' and thou shalt share Treasures of Babylon."

The Tale of The Gold Lender of Babylon

FIFTY PIECES OF GOLD! Never before had Rodan, the spearmaker of old Babylon, carried so much gold in his leather wallet. Happily down the king's highway from the palace of his most liberal Majesty he strode. Cheerfully the gold clinked as the wallet at his belt swayed with each step the sweetest music he had ever heard.

Fifty pieces of gold! All his! He could hardly realize his good fortune. What power in those clinking discs! They could purchase anything he wanted, a grand house, land, cattle, camels, horses, chariots, whatever he might desire.

What use should he make of it? This evening as he turned into a side street towards the home of his sister, he could think of nothing he would rather possess than those same glittering, heavy pieces of gold – his to keep.

It was upon an evening some days later that a perplexed Rodan entered the shop of Mathon, the lender of gold and dealer in jewels and rare fabrics. Glancing neither to the right nor the left at the colorful articles artfully displayed, he passed through to the living quarters at the rear. Here he found the genteel Mathon lounging upon a rug partaking of a meal served by a black slave.

"I would counsel with thee for I know not what to do." Rodan stood stolidly, feet apart, hairy breast exposed by the gaping front of his leather jacket.

Mathon's narrow, sallow face smiled a friendly greeting. "What indiscretions hast thou done that thou shouldst seek the lender of gold? Hast been unlucky at the gaming table? Or hath some lump dame entangled thee? For many years have I known thee, yet never before hast thou sought me to aid thee in thy troubles."

"No, no. Not such as that. I seek no gold. Instead I crave thy wise advice."

"Hear! Hear! What this man doth say. No one comes to the lender of gold for advice. My ears must play me false."

"They listen true."

"Can this be so? Rodan, the spearmaker, doth display more cunning than all the rest, for he comes to Mathon, not for gold, but for advice. Many men come to me for gold to pay for their follies, but as for advice, they want it not.

Yet who is more able to advise than the lender of gold to whom many men come in trouble?

"Thou shalt eat with me, Rodan," he continued. "Thou shalt be my guest for the evening. Ando!" he commanded of the black slave, "draw up a rug for my friend, Rodan the spearmaker, who comes for advice. He shall be mine honored guest. Bring to him much food and get for him my largest cup. Choose well of the best wine that he may have satisfaction in the drinking.

"Tell me what troubles thee."

"It is the king's gift."

"The king's gift? The king did make thee a gift and it gives thee trouble? What manner of gift?"

"Because he was much pleased with the design I did submit to him for a new point on the spears of the royal guard, he did present me with fifty pieces of gold, and now I am much perplexed. I am beseeched each hour the sun doth travel across the sky by those who would share it with me."

"That is natural. More men want gold than have it, and would wish one who comes by it easily to divide. But can you not say 'No'? Is thy will not as strong as thy fist?"

'To many I can say no, yet sometimes it would be easier to say yes. Can one refuse to share with one's only sister to whom he is deeply devoted?"

"Surely, thy own sister would not wish to deprive thee of enjoying thy reward."

"But it is for the sake of Araman, her husband, whom she wishes to see a rich merchant.

She does feel that he has never had a chance and she beseeches me to loan to him this gold that he may become a prosperous merchant and repay me from his profits."

"My friend," resumed Mathon, "'tis a worthy subject thou bringest to discuss. Gold bringeth unto its possessor responsibility and a changed position with his fellow men. It bringeth fear lest he lose it or it be tricked away from him. It bringeth a feeling of power and ability to do good. Likewise, it bringeth opportunities whereby his very good intentions may bring him into difficulties. Didst ever hear of the farmer of Nineveh who could understand the language of animals? I wot not for 'tis not the kind of tale men like thee tell over the bronze caster's forge. I will tell it to thee for thou shouldst know that to borrowing and lending there is more than the passing of gold from the hands of one to the hands of another.

"This farmer who could understand what the animals said to each other, did linger in the farm yard each evening just to listen to their words. One evening he did hear the ox bemoaning to the ass the hardness of his lot. 'I do labor pulling the plow from morning until night. No matter how hot the day, or how tired my legs, or how the bow doth chafe my neck, still must I work. But you are a creature of leisure. You are trapped with a colorful blanket and do nothing more than carry our master about where he wishes to go. When he goes nowhere you do rest and eat the green grass all the day'.

"Now the ass, in spite of his vicious heels, was a goodly fellow and sympathized with the ox. 'My good friend', he replied, 'you do work very hard and I would help ease your lot. Therefore, will I tell you how you may have a day of rest. In the morning when the slave comes to fetch you to the plow, lie upon the ground and bellow much that he may say you are sick and cannot work'.

"So the ox took the advice of the ass and the next morning the slave returned to the farmer and told him the ox was sick and could not pull the plow.

"'Then', said the farmer, 'hitch the ass to the plow for the plowing must go on'.

"All that day the ass, who had only intended to help his friend, found himself compelled to do the ox's task. When night came and he was released from the plow his heart was bitter and his legs were weary and his neck was sore where the bow had chafed it.

'The farmer lingered in the barnyard to listen.

'The ox began first. 'You are my good friend. Because of your wise advice I have enjoyed a day of rest'.

"And I," retorted the ass, 'am like many another simple hearted one who starts to help a friend and ends up by doing his task for him. Hereafter you draw your own plow, for I did hear the master tell the slave to send for the butcher were you sick again. I wish he would, for you are a lazy fellow'. Thereafter they spoke to each other no more this ended their friendship. Canst thou tell the moral to this tale, Rodan?"

"'Tis a good tale," responded Rodan, "but I see not the moral."

"I thought not that you would. But it is there and simple too. Just this: If thou desire to help thy friend, do so in a way that will not bring thy friend's burdens upon thyself."

"I had not thought of that. It is a wise moral. I wish not to assume the burdens of my sister's husband. But tell me. You lend to many. Do not the borrowers repay?"

Mathon smiled the smile of one whose soul is rich with much experience. "Could a loan be well made if the borrower cannot repay? Must not the lender be wise and judge carefully whether his gold can perform a useful purpose to the borrower and return to him once more; or whether it will be wasted by one unable to use it wisely and leave him with out his treasure, and leave the borrower with a debt he cannot repay? I will show to thee the tokens in my token chest and let them tell thee some of their stories."

Into the room he brought a chest as long as his arm covered with red pigskin and ornamented with bronze designs. He placed it upon the floor and squatted before it, both hands upon the lid.

'From each person to whom I lend, I do exact a token for my token chest, to remain there until the loan is repaid. When they re pay I give back, but if they never repay it will always remind me of one who was not faithful to my confidence.

'The safest loans, my token box tells me, are to those whose possessions are of more value than the loan they desire. They own lands or jewels, or camels, or other things which could be sold to repay the loan. Some of the tokens given to me are jewels of more value than the loan. Others are promises that if the loan be not repaid as agreed they will deliver to me certain property in settlement. On loans like those I am assured that my gold will be returned with the rental thereon, for the loan is based on property.

"In another class are those who have the capacity to earn. They are such as you, who labor or serve and are paid. They have income and if they are honest and suffer no misfortune, I know that they can also repay the gold I loan them and the rental to which I am entitled. Such loans are based on human effort.

"Others are those who have neither property nor assured earning capacity. Life is hard and there will always be some who cannot adjust themselves to it. Alas for the loans I make them, even though they be no larger than a pence, my token box may censure me in the years to come unless they be guaranteed by good friends of the borrower who know him honorable."

Mathon released the clasp and opened the lid. Rodan leaned forward eagerly.

At the top of the chest a bronze neck piece lay upon a scarlet cloth. Mathon picked up the piece and patted it affectionately. "'This shall always remain in my token chest because the owner has passed on into the great darkness. I treasure it, his token, and I treasure his memory; for he was my good friend. We traded together with much success until out of the east he brought a woman to wed, beautiful, but not like our women. A dazzling creature. He spent his gold lavishly to gratify her desires. He came to me in distress when his gold was gone. I counselled with him. I told him I would help him to once more master his own affairs. He swore by the sign of the Great Bull that he would. But it was not to be. In a quarrel she thrust a knife into the heart he dared her to pierce."

"And she?" questioned Rodan.

"Yes, of course, this was hers." He picked up the scarlet cloth. "In bitter remorse she threw herself into the Euphrates. These two loans will never be repaid. The chest tells you, Rodan, that humans in the throws of great emotions are not safe risks for the gold lender.

"Here! Now this is different." He reached for a ring carved of ox bone. "This belongs to a farmer. I buy the rugs of his women. The locusts came and they had not food. I helped him and when the new crop came he repaid me. Later he came again and told of strange goats in a distant land as described by a traveler. They had long hair so fine and soft it would weave into rugs more beautiful than any ever seen in Babylon. He wanted a herd but he had no money. So I did lend him gold to make the journey and bring back goats. Now his herd is begun and next year I shall surprise the lords of Babylon with the most expensive rugs it has been their good fortune to buy. Soon I must return his ring. He doth insist on repaying promptly."

"Some borrowers do that?" queried Rodan.

"If they borrow for purposes that bring money back to them, I find it so. But if they borrow because of their indiscretions, I warn thee to be cautious if thou wouldst ever have thy gold back in hand again."

'Tell me about this," requested Rodan, picking up a heavy gold bracelet inset with jewels in rare designs.

"The women do appeal to my good friend," bantered Mathon.

"I am so much younger than you," retorted Rodan.

"I grant that, but this time thou doth suspicion romance where it is not. The owner of this is fat and wrinkled and doth talk so much and say so little she drives me mad. Once they had much money and were my good customers, but ill times came upon them. She has a son of whom she would make a merchant. So she came to me and borrowed gold so that he might become a partner of a caravan owner who travels with his camels bartering in one city what he buys in another.

'This man proved a rascal for he left the poor boy in a distant city without money and without friends, pulling out early while the youth slept. Perhaps when this youth has grown to manhood, he will repay; until then I get no rental for the loan – only much talk. But I do admit the jewels are worthy of the loan."

"Did this lady ask thy advice as to the wisdom of the loan?"

"Quite otherwise. She had pictured to herself this son of hers as a wealthy and powerful man of Babylon. To suggest the contrary was to infuriate her. A fair rebuke I had. I knew the risk for this inexperienced boy, but as she offered security I could not refuse her.

'This," continued Mathon, waving a bit of pack rope tied into a knot, "belongs to Nebatur, the camel trader. When he would buy a herd larger than his funds he brings to me this knot and I lend to him according to his needs. He is a wise trader. I have confidence in his good judgment and can lend him freely. Many other merchants of Babylon have my confidence because of their honorable behavior. Their tokens come and go frequently in my token box. Good merchants are an asset to our city and it profits me to aid them to keep trade moving that Babylon be prosperous."

Mathon picked out a beetle carved in turquoise and tossed it contemptuously. "A bug from Egypt. The lad who owns this does not care whether I ever receive back my gold; When I reproach him he replies, 'How can I repay when ill fate pursues me? You have plenty more'. What can I do, the token is his father's – a worthy man of small means who did pledge his land and herd to back his son's enterprises. The youth found success at first and then was overzealous to gain great wealth. His knowledge was immature. His enterprises collapsed.

"Youth is ambitious. Youth would take cuts to wealth and the desirable things for which it stands. To secure wealth quickly youth often borrows unwisely. Youth never having had experience cannot realize that hopeless debt is like a deep pit into which one may descend quickly and where one may struggle vainly for many days.

It is a pit of sorrow and regrets where the brightness of the sun is overcast and night is made unhappy by restless sleeping. Yet, I do not discourage borrowing gold. I encourage it. I recommend it if it for a wise purpose. I myself made my first success as a merchant with borrowed gold.

"Yet, what should the lender do in such a situation. The youth is in despair and accomplishes nothing. He is discouraged. He makes no effort to repay. My heart turns against depriving the father of his land and cattle."

"You tell me much that I am interested to hear," ventured Rodan, "but, I hear no answer to my question. Should I lend my fifty pieces of gold to my sister's husband? They mean much to me."

"Thy sister is a sterling woman whom I do much esteem. Should her husband come to me and ask to borrow fifty pieces of gold I should ask him for what purpose he would use it.

"If he answered that he desired to become a merchant like myself and deal in jewels and rich furnishings, I would say, 'What knowledge have you of the ways of trade? Do you know where you can buy at lowest cost? Do you know where you can sell at a fair price? Could he say 'Yes' to these questions?"

"No, he could not," Rodan admitted. "He has helped me much in making spears and he has helped some in the shops."

'Then, would I say to him that his purpose was not wise. Merchants must learn their trade. His ambition, though worthy, is not practical and I would not lend him any gold. "But, supposing he could say, 'Yes, I have helped merchants much. I know how to travel to Smyrna and to buy at low cost the rugs the housewives weave. I also know many of the rich people of Babylon to whom I can sell these at a large profit.' Then I would say: 'Your purpose is wise and your ambition honorable. I shall be glad to lend you the fifty pieces of gold if you can give me security that they will be returned' But would he say, 'I have no security other than that I am an honored man and will pay you well for the loan.' Then would I reply, 'I treasure much each piece of gold. Were the robbers to take it from you as you journeyed to Smyrna or take the rugs from you as you returned, then you would have no means of repaying me and my gold would be gone!'

"Gold, you see, Rodan, is the merchandise of the lender of money. It is easy to lend. If it is lent unwisely then it is difficult to get back. The wise lender wishes not the risk of the undertaking but the guarantee of safe repayment.

"'Tis well," he continued, "to assist those that are in trouble, 'tis well to help those upon whom fate has laid a heavy hand. 'Tis well to help those who are starting that they may progress and become valuable citizens. But help must be given wisely, lest, like the farmer's ass, in our desire to help we but take upon ourselves the burden that belongs to another.

"Again I wandered from thy question, Rodan, but hear my answer: Keep thy fifty pieces of gold. What thy labor earns for thee and what is given thee for reward is thine own and no man can put an obligation upon thee to part with it unless it do be thy wish. If wouldst lent it so that it may earn thee more gold, then lend with caution and in many places. I like not idle gold, and even less I like too much of risk."

"How many years hast thou labored as a spearmaker?"

"Fully three."

"How much besides the King's gift hast saved?"

"Three gold pieces."

"Each year that thou hast labored thou hast denied thyself good things to save from thine earnings one piece of gold?"

"Tis as you say."

'Then mightest save in fifty years of labor fifty pieces of gold by thy self denial?"

"A lifetime of labor it would be."

"Thinkest thou thy sister would wish to jeopardize the savings of fifty years of labor over the bronze melting pot that her husband might experiment on being a merchant?"

"Not if I spoke in your words."

"Then go to her and say, 'Three years I have labored each day except fast days, from morning until night, and I have denied myself many things that my heart craved. For each year of labor and self denial I have to show one piece of gold. Thou art my favored sister and I wish that thy husband may engage in business in which he will prosper greatly. If he will submit to me a plan that seems wise and possible to my friend, Mathon, then will I gladly lend to him my savings of an entire year that he may have an opportunity to prove that he can succeed.' Do that, I say, and if he has within him the soul to succeed he can prove it. If he fails he will not owe thee more than he can hope to some day repay.

"I am a gold lender because I own more gold than I can use in my own trade. I desire my surplus gold to labor for others and thereby earn more gold. I do not wish to take risk of losing my gold for I have labored much and denied myself much to secure it. Therefore, I will no longer lend any of it where I am not confident that it is safe and will be returned to me. Neither will I lend it where I am not convinced that its earnings will be promptly paid to me.

"I have told to thee, Rodan, a few of the secrets of my token chest. From them you may understand the weakness of men and their eagerness to borrow that which they have no certain means to repay. From this you can see how often their high hopes of the great earnings they could make, if they but had gold, are but false hopes they have not the ability or training to fulfill.

"Thou, Rodan, now have gold which thou shouldst put to earning more gold for thee. Thou art about to become even as I, a gold lender. If thou dost safely preserve thy treasure it will produce liberal earnings for thee and be a rich source of pleasure and profit during all thy days. But if thou dost let it escape from thee, it will be a source of constant sorrow and regret as long as thy memory doth last.

"What desirest thou most of this gold in thy wallet?"

'To keep it safe.'

"Wisely spoken," replied Mathon approvingly. 'Thy first desire is for safety. Thinkest thou that in the custody of thy sister's husband it would be truly safe from possible loss?"

"I fear not, for he is not wise in guarding gold."

"Then be not swayed by foolish sentiments of obligation to trust thy treasure to any person. If thou wouldst help thy family or thy friends, find other ways than risking the loss of thy treasure. Forget not that gold slippeth away in unexpected ways from those unskilled in guarding it. As well waste thy treasure in extravagance as let others lose it for thee.

"What next after safety dost desire of this treasure of thine?"

'That it earn more gold.'

"Again thou speakest with wisdom. It should be made to earn and grow larger. Gold wisely lent may even double itself with its earnings before a man like you groweth old. If you risk losing it you risk losing all that it would earn as well.

"Therefore, be not swayed by the fantastic plans of impractical men who think they see ways to force thy gold to make earnings un. usually large. Such plans are the creations of dreamers unskilled in the safe and dependable laws of trade. Be conservative in what thou expect it to earn that thou mayest keep and enjoy thy treasure. To hire it out with a promise of usurious returns is to invite loss.

"Seek to associate thyself with men and enterprises whose success is established that thy treasure may earn liberally under their skillful use and be guarded safely by their wisdom and experience.

"Thus, mayest thou avoid the misfortunes follow most of the sons of men to whom God sees fit to entrust gold."

When Rodan would thank him for his wise advice he would not listen, saying, "The king's gift shall teach thee much wisdom. If wouldst keep thy fifty pieces of gold thou must be discreet indeed. Many uses will tempt thee. Much advice will be spoken to thee. Numerous opportunities to make large profits will be offered thee. The stories from my token box should warn thee, before thou let any piece of gold leave thy pouch to be sure that thou hast a safe way to pull it back again. Should my further advice appeal to thee, return again. It is gladly given.

"Ere thou goest read this which I have carved beneath the lid of my token box. It applies equally to the borrower and the lender:

"Better a Little Caution than a Great Regret".

The Tale of The Walls of Babylon

OLD BANZAR, grim-warrior of another day, stood guard at the passageway leading to the top of the ancient walls of Babylon.

Up above, valiant defenders were battling to hold the walls. Upon them depended the future existence of this great city with its hundreds of thousands of citizens.

Over the walls came the roar of the attacking armies, the yelling of many men, the trampling of thousands of horses, the deafening boom of the battering rams pounding the bronzed gates.

In the street behind the gate, lounged the spearmen, awaiting to defend the entrance should the gates give way. They were but a few of the task. The main armies of Babylon were with their king, far away in the east upon the great expedition against the Elamites. No attack upon the city being anticipated during their absence, the defending forces were small. Unexpectedly from the north bore down the mighty armies of the Assyrians. The walls must hold or Babylon was doomed.

About Banzar were great crowds of citizens, white faced and terrified, eagerly seeking news of the battle. With hushed awe they viewed the stream of wounded and dead being carried or led out of the passageway.

Here was the crucial point of attack. After three days of circling about the city, the enemy had suddenly thrown his great strength against this section and this gate.

The defenders from the top of the wall fought off the climbing platforms and the scaling ladders of the attackers with arrows, burning oil and lastly spears, if any reached the top. Against the defenders, thousands of the enemies' archers poured a deadly barrage of arrows.

Old Banzar had the vantage point for news. He was closest to the conflict and first to hear of each fresh repulse of the frenzied attackers.

An elderly merchant crowded close to him, his palsied hands quivering. "Tell me! Tell me!" he pleaded. "They cannot get in. My sons are with the good king. There is no one to protect my old wife. My goods, they will steal all. My food, they will leave nothing. We are old, too old to defend ourselves – too old for slaves. We shall starve. We shall die. Tell me they cannot get in."

"Calm thyself, good merchant," the guard responded. 'The walls of Babylon are strong. Go back to the bazaar and tell your wife that the walls will protect you and all of your possessions as safely as they protect the rich treasures of the king. Keep close to the walls, lest the arrows flying over, strike you!"

A woman with a babe in arms took the old man's place as he withdrew.
"Sergeant, what news from the top? Tell me truly that I may reassure my poor hus-

band. He lies with fever from his terrible wounds, yet insists upon his armor and his spear to protect me, who am with child. Terrible he says will be the vengeful lust of our enemies should they break in."

"Be thou of good heart, thou mother that is, and is again to be, the walls of Babylon will protect you and your babes. They are high and strong. Hear ye not the yells of our valiant defenders as they empty the caldrons of burning oil upon the ladder scalers?"

"Yes, that do I hear and also the roar of the battering rams that do hammer at our gates."

"Back to thy husband. Tell him the gates are strong and withstand the rams. Also that the scalers climb the walls but to receive the waiting spear thrust. Watch thy way and hasten behind yon buildings."

Banzar stepped aside to clear the passage for heavily armed reinforcements. As with clanking bronze shields and heavy tread they tramped by, a small girl plucked at his girdle.

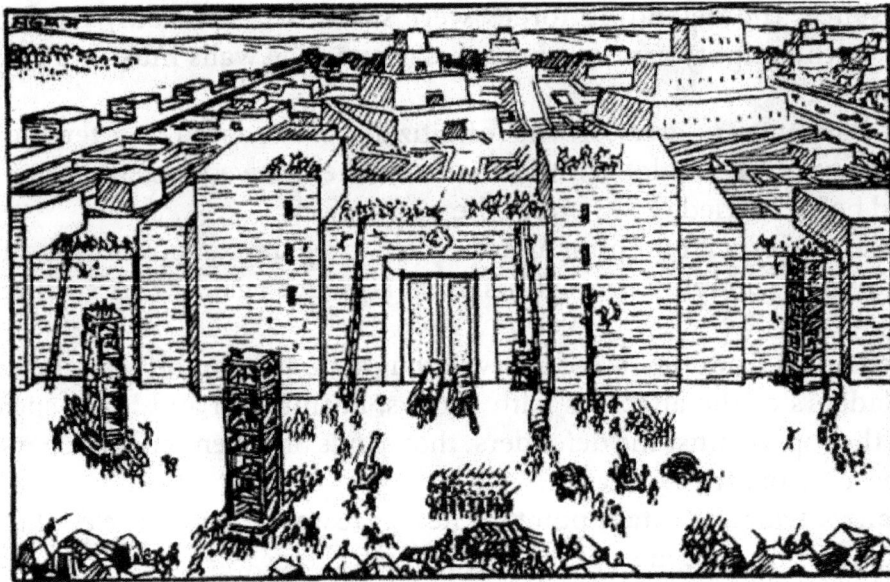

"Tell me please, soldier, are we safe?" she pleaded. "I hear the awful noises. I see the men all bleeding. I am so frightened. What will become of our family, of my mother, little brother and the baby?"

The grim old campaigner blinked his eyes and thrust forward his chin as he beheld the child.

"Be not afraid, little one," he reassured her. "The walls of Babylon will protect you and mother and little brother and the baby. It was for the safety of such as you that the good Queen Semiramis built them over a hundred years ago. Never have they been broken through. Go back and tell your mother and little brother and the baby that the walls of Babylon will protect them and they need have no fear."

Day after day old Banzar stood at his post and watched the reinforcements up the passageway, there to stay and fight until wounded or dead they came down once more. Around him, unceasingly crowded the throngs of frightened citizens eagerly seeking to learn if the walls would hold. To all he gave his answer with the fine dignity of an old soldier. "The walls of Babylon will protect you."

For three weeks and five days the attack waged with scarcely ceasing violence. Harder and grimmer set the jaw of Banzar as the passage behind, wet with the blood of the many wounded, was churned into mud by the never ceasing streams of men passing up and staggering down. Each day the slaughtered attackers piled up in heaps before the wall. Each night they were carried back and buried by their comrades.

Upon the fifth night of the fourth week the clamor without diminished. The first streaks of daylight illuminating the plains disclosed great clouds of dust raised by the retreating armies.

A mighty shout went up from the defenders. There was no mistake in its meaning. It was repeated by the waiting troops behind the walls. It was echoed by the citizens upon the street. It swept over the city with the violence of a storm.

People rushed from the houses. The streets were jammed with a throbbing mob. The pent up fear of weeks found an outlet in the wild chorus of joy. From the top of the high tower of the Temple of Bel burst forth the flames of victory. Skyward floated the column of blue smoke to carry the message far and wide.

The walls of Babylon had once again repulsed a mighty and vicious foe determined to loot her rich treasures and to ravish and enslave her citizens.

Babylon endured century after century because it was FULLY PROTECTED. It could not afford to be otherwise.

The walls of Babylon were an outstanding example of man's need and desire for protection. This desire is inherent in the human race. It is just as strong today as it ever was, but we have developed broader and better plans to accomplish the same purpose.

In this day, behind the impregnable walls of insurance, savings accounts and dependable investments, we can guard ourselves against the unexpected tragedies that may enter any door and seat themselves before any fireside. We cannot afford to be without adequate protection.

The Tale of The Camel Trader of Babylon

THE hungrier one becomes the clearer one's mind works, also the more sensitive one becomes to the odors of food.

For two days Tarkad, the son of Azure, had tasted no food except for two small figs purloined from over the wall of a garden before an angry Babylonian housekeeper chased him down the street. The woman's cries still rang in his ears and restrained his restless fingers from snatching tempting fruits from the baskets of the market women between who he strolled.

He paced back and forth before the eating house hoping to meet someone he knew; someone from whom he could borrow a bit of copper that would gain him a friendly smile and a liberal helping from the fat keeper. Without the copper he knew how unwelcome he would be.

In his abstraction he unexpectedly found himself face to face with the tall bony figure of Dabasir, the camel trader.

"Ha! 'Tis Tarkad, whom I have been seeking that he might repay to me the two pieces of copper which I lent to him a moon ago and the piece of silver which I lent to him before that. We are well met. I can make good use of the coin this very day. What say, boy? What say?"

Tarkad stuttered and his face flushed. He had little desire to encounter the outspoken Dabasir. "I am sorry, very sorry, but this day I have not the copper nor the silver with which I could repay."

"But get it then! Surely thou canst get a few coppers and a piece of silver to repay the generosity of an old friend of thy father who aided thee whenst thou wast in need?"

" 'Tis because ill fortune does pursue me that I cannot repay."

"Ill fortune! Wouldst blame God for thine own weakness. Ill fortune pursues every man who thinks more of borrowing than of repaying. Come with me, boy, while I eat. I am hungry and I would tell thee a tale."

Tarkad flinched from the brutal frankness of Dabasir, but here at least was an invitation to enter the coveted doorway of the eating house.

Dabasir pushed him to a far corner of the room where they seated themselves upon small rugs.

When Kauskor, the proprietor, appeared smiling, Dabasir addressed him with his usual freedom. "Fat lizard of the desert, bring to me a leg of the goat very brown with much juice and bread and all of the vegetables for I am hungry and want much food. Do not forget my friend here. Bring to him a jug of water. Have it cooled, for the day is hot."

Tarkad's heart sank. Must he sit here and drink water while he watched this man devour an entire goat leg? He said nothing. He thought of nothing he could say.

Dabasir, however, knew no such thing as silence. Smiling and waving his hand good-naturedly to the other customers, all of whom knew him, he continued.

"I did hear from a traveller just returned from Urfa of a certain rich man who has a piece of stone cut so thin that one can look through it. He put it in the window of his house to keep out the rains. It is yellow so this traveller does relate, and he was permitted to look through it and all the outside world looked strange and not like it really is. What say you to that, Tarkad? Thinkest all the world could look to a man a different color what what it is?"

"I dare say," responded the youth, much more interested in the fat leg of goat placed before Dabasir.

"Well, I know it for I myself have seen the world all a different color from what it really is and the tale I am about to tell relates how I came to see it in its right color once more."

"Dabasir will tell a tale," whispered a neighboring diner to his neighbor, and dragged his rug close. Other diners brought their food and crowded in a semi circle. They crunched noisily in the ears of Tarkad and brushed him with their meaty bones. He alone was without food. Dabasir did not offer to share with him nor even motion him to a small corner of the hard bread that was broken off and had fallen from the platter to the floor.

"The tale that I am about to tell," began Dabasir, pausing to bite a goodly chunk from the goat leg, "relates to my early life and how I came to be a camel trader. Didst anyone know that I once was a slave in Syria?"

A murmur of surprise ran through the audience to which Dabasir listened with satisfaction.

"When I was a young man," continued Dabasir after another vicious onslaught on the goat leg, "I learned the trade of my father, the making of saddles. I worked with him in his shop and took to myself a wife. Being young and not greatly skilled, I could earn but little, just enough to support my excellent wife in a modest way. I craved good things which I could not afford. Soon I found that the shop keepers would trust me to pay later even though I could not pay at the time. So I indulged my desires and wore fine raiment and bought many things for my wife and my home beyond the reach of my earnings. I paid as I could and for a while all went well. But in time I discovered I could not use my earnings both to live upon and to pay my debts. Creditors began to pursue me to pay for my extravagant purchases and my life became miserable. I borrowed from my friends, but could not repay them either. Things went from bad to worse. My wife returned to her father and I decided to leave Babylon and seek another city where as I thought a young man might have a chance to succeed.

"For two years I led a restless and unsuccessful life working for caravan traders. From this I fell in with a set of likeable robbers who scoured the desert for unarmed caravans. Such deeds were unworthy of the son of my father, but I was seeing the world through a colored stone and did not realize to what degradation I had fallen.

"We met with success on our first trip, capturing a rich haul of gold and silks and valuable merchandise. This loot we took to Ginir and squandered. The second time we were not so fortunate. Just after we had made our capture, we were attacked by the spearsmen of a native chief to whom the caravans paid for protection. Our two leaders were killed and the rest of us were taken to Damascus where we were stripped of our clothing and sold as slaves.

"I was purchased for two pieces of silver by a Syrian desert chief. With my hair shorn and but a loin cloth to wear, I was not so different from the other slaves. Being a reckless youth, I thought it merely an adventure until my master took me before his four wives and told them they could have me for a eunuch.

"Then, indeed, did I realize the hopelessness of my situation. These men of the desert were fierce and warlike. I was subject to their will without weapons or means of escape.

"Fearful I stood, as those four women looked me over. I wondered if I could expect pity from them. Sira, the first wife, was older than the others. Her face was impassive as she looked upon me. I turned from her with little consolation. The next was a contemptuous beauty who gazed at me as indifferently as if I had been a worm of the earth. The two younger ones tittered as though it were all an exciting joke.

It seemed an age that I stood waiting sentence. Each woman appeared willing for the others to decide. Finally Sira spoke up in a cold voice.

"Of eunuchs we have plenty, but of camel tenders we have few and they are a worthless lot. Even this day I would visit my mother who is sick with the fever and there is no slave I would trust to lead my camel. Ask this slave if he can lead a camel."

"My master thereupon questioned me. 'What know you of camels?'

"Striving to conceal my eagerness, I replied, 'I can make them kneel, I can load them, I can lead them on long trips without tiring. If need be, I can repair their trappings.'

"'The slave speaks forward enough,' observed my master. 'If thou so desire, Sira, take this man for thy camel tender.'

"So I was turned over to Sira and that day I led her camel upon a long journey to her sick mother. I took the occasion to thank her for her intercession and also to tell her that I was not a slave by birth, but the son of a freeman, an honorable saddle maker of Babylon. I also told her much of my story. Her comments were disconcerting to me and I pondered much afterwards on what she said.

"How can you call yourself a free man when your weakness has brought you to this? If a man has in himself the soul of a slave will he not become one no matter what his birth, even as water seeks its level? If a man has within him the soul of a free man, will he not become respected and honored in his own city in spite of his misfortune?'

"For over a year I was a slave and lived with the slaves, but I could not become as one of them. One day Sira asked me, 'In the even, time when the other slaves can mingle and enjoy the society of each other thy tent alone?'

"To which I responded, 'I am pondering what you have said to me. I wonder if I have the soul of a slave. I cannot join them, so I must sit apart.'

'I, too, must sit apart', she confided. 'My dowry was large and my lord married me be cause of it. Yet he does not desire me. What every woman longs for is to be desired. Because of this and because I am barren and have neither son nor daughter, must I sit apart. Were I a man I would rather die than be such a slave, but the conventions of our tribe make slaves of women.'

"Have I the soul of a man or have I the soul of a slave? What think you?' I asked.

"'Have you a desire to repay the just debts you owe in Babylon?'

"Yes, I have the desire, but I see no way.'

"'If thou contentedly let the years slip by and make no effort to repay, then thou hast but the contemptible soul of a slave. No man is otherwise who cannot respect himself and no man can respect himself who does not repay honest debts.'

"But what can I do who am a slave in Syria?"

"Stay a slave in Syria, thou weakling.'

"I am not a weakling', I denied hotly.

"Then prove it.'

"How?"

"Dost not thy great king fight his enemies in every way he can and with every force he has? Thy debts are thy enemies that have run thee out of Babylon. You left them alone and they grew too strong for thee. Hadst fought them as a man, thou couldst have conquered them and been one, honored among thy townspeople. But thou had not the soul to fight them and behold thou hast gone down until thou art a slave in Syria.'

"Much I thought over her unkind accusations and many defensive phrases I worded to prove myself not a slave at heart, but I was not to have the chance to use them. Three days later the maid of Sira took me to her mistress.

'My mother is again very sick', she said. 'Saddle the two best camels in my husband's herd. Tie on water skins and saddle bags for a long journey. The maid will give thee food at the kitchen tent.' I packed the camels, wondering much at the quantity of provision the maid provided, for the mother dwelt less than a day's journey away. The maid rode the rear camel which followed and I led the camel of my mistress. When we reached her mother's house it was just dark. Sira dismissed the maid and said to me:

"Hast thou the soul of a free man or the soul of a slave?'

"The soul of a free man', I responded.

"Now is thy chance to prove it. Thy master hath imbibed deeply and his chiefs are in a stupor. Take then these camels and make thy escape. Here in this bag is raiment of thy master's to disguise thee. I will say thou stole the camels and ran away while I visited my sick mother."

"Thou hast the soul of a queen," I told her. 'Much do I wish that I might lead thee to happiness.'

"'Happiness', she responded, 'awaits not the runaway wife who seeks it in far lands among strange people. Go thy own way and may God of the desert protect thee for the way is far and barren of food or water.'

"I needed no further urging, but thanked her warmly and was away into the night. I knew not this strange country and had only a dim idea of the direction in which lay Babylon, but struck out bravely across the desert toward the hills. One camel I rode and the other I led. All that night I traveled and all the next day, urged on by the knowledge of the terrible fate that was meted out to slaves who stole their master's property and tried to escape.

"Late that afternoon, I reached a rough country as uninhabitable as the desert. The sharp rocks bruised the feet of my faithful camels and soon they were picking their way slowly and painfully along. I met neither man nor beast and could well understand why they shunned this inhospitable land.

"It was such a journey from then on as few men live to tell of. Day after day we plodded along. Food and water gave out. The heat of the sun was merciless. At the end of the ninth day, I slid from the back of my mount with the feeling that I was too weak to ever remount and I would surely die, lost in this abandoned country.

"I stretched out upon the ground and slept, not waking until the first gleam of daylight.

"I sat up and looked about me. There was a coolness in the morning air. My camels lay dejected not far away. About me was a vast waste of broken country covered with rock and sand and thorny things, no sign of water, naught to eat for man or camel.

"Could it be that in this peaceful quiet I faced my end? My mind was clearer than it had ever been before. My body now seemed of little importance. My parched and bleeding lips, my dry and swollen tongue, my empty stomach, all had lost their supreme importance of the day before.

"I looked across into the uninviting distance and once again came to me the question, 'Have I the soul of a slave or the soul of a free man?' Then with clearness I realized that if I had the soul of a slave, I should give up, lie down in the desert and die, a fitting end for a runaway slave.

"But if I had the soul of a free man, what then? Surely I would force my way back to Babylon, repay the people who had trusted me, bring happiness to my wife who had cared for me, bring peace and contentment to my parents.

"'Thy debts are thine enemies who have run thee out of Babylon', Sira had said. Yes, it was so. Why had I refused to stand my ground like a man? Why had I permitted my wife to go back to her father? Why had I been weak like a slave if I had not the soul of one?

'Then a strange thing happened. All the world seemed to be of a different color as though I had been looking at it through a colored stone which had suddenly been removed. At last I saw the true values in life.

"Die in the desert! Not I! With a new vision, I saw the things that I must do. First I would go back to Babylon and face every man to whom I owed an unpaid debt. I should tell them that after years of wandering and misfortune, I had come back to pay my debts as fast as God would permit. Next I should make a home for my wife and become a citizen of whom my parents should be proud.

"My debts were my enemies, but the men I owed were my friends for they had trusted me and believed in me.

"I staggered weakly to my feet. What mattered hunger? What mattered thirst? They were but incidents on the road to Babylon. Within me surged the soul of a free man going back to conquer his enemies and reward his friends. I thrilled with the great resolve.

"The glazed eyes of my camels brightened at the new note in my husky voice. With great effort, after many attempts, they gained their feet. With pitiful perseverance, they pushed on toward the north where something within me said we would find Babylon.

"We found water. We passed into a more fertile country where were grass and fruit. We found the trail to Babylon because the soul of a free man looks at life as a series of problems to be solved and solves them, while the soul of a slave whines, 'What can I do who am but a slave?'

"How about thee, Tarkad? Dost thy empty stomach make thy head exceedingly clear? Art ready to take the road that leads to Babylon?"

Moisture came to the eyes of the youth. He rose eagerly to his knees. 'Thou hast shown me a vision; already I feel the soul of a free man surge within me."

Again Dabasir turned to his food. "Kauskor, thou snail", he called loudly to be heard in the kitchen, "the food is cold. Bring me more meat fresh from the roasting. Bring thou also a portion for Tarkad the son of my old friend who is hungry and shall eat with me."

So ended the tale of Dabasir the camel trader of old Babylon. He found his own soul when he realized a great truth, a truth that had been known and used by wise men long before his time.

It has led men of all ages out of difficulties and into success and it will continue to do so for those who have the wisdom to understand its magic power. It is for any man to use who reads these lines.

Where the Determination is, the Way Can Be Found

The Tale of The Clay Tablets from Babylon

ST. SWITHIN'S COLLEGE
NOTTINGHAM UNIVERSITY
NEWARK-ON-TRENT
NOTTINGHAM

October 21,1934.

Professor Franklin Caldwell,
Care of British Scientific Expedition,
Hillah, Mesopotamia.

My dear Professor:

The five clay tablets from your recent excavation in the ruins of Babylon arrived on the same boat with your letter. I have been fascinated no end, and have spent many pleasant hours translating their inscriptions. I should have answered your letter at once but delayed until I could complete the translations which are attached.

The tablets arrived without damage, thanks to your careful use of preservatives and excellent packing.

You will be as astonished as we in the laboratory, at the story they relate. One expects the dim and distant past to speak of romance and adventure. "Arabian Nights" sort of things, you know. When instead it discloses the problem of a person named Dabasir to pay off his debts, one realizes that conditions upon this old world have not changed as much in five thousand years as one might expect.

It's odd, you know, but these old inscriptions rather 'rag' me, as the students say. Being a college professor, I am supposed to be a thinking human being possessing a working knowledge upon most subjects. Yet, here comes this old chap out of the dust-covered ruins of Babylon to offer a way I had never heard of, to pay off my debts and at the same time acquire gold to jingle in my wallet.

Pleasant thought, I say, and interesting to prove whether it will work as well nowadays as it did in old Babylon. Mrs. Shrewsbury and myself are planning to try out his plan upon our own affairs which could be much improved.

Wishing you the best of luck in your worthy undertaking and waiting eagerly another opportunity to assist, I am,

> Yours sincerely,
> Alfred H. Shrewsbury,
> Department of Archaeology.

TABLET Nº. 1

Now when the moon becometh full I, Dabasir, who am but recently returned from slavery in Syria, with the determination to pay my many just debts and become a man of means worthy of respect in my native city of Babylon, do here engrave upon the clay a permanent record of my affairs to guide and assist me in carrying through my high desires.

Under the wise advice of my good friend Mathon, the gold lender, I am determined to follow an exact plan that he doth say will lead any honorable man out of debt into means and self respect.

This plan includeth three purposes which are my hope and desire.

First, the PLAN doth provide for my future prosperity.

Therefore one-tenth of all I earn shall be set aside as my own to keep. For Mathon speaketh wisely when he saith:

"That man who keepeth in his purse both gold and silver that he need not spend is good to his family and loyal to his king.

"The man who hath but a few coppers in his purse, is indifferent to his family and indifferent to his king.

"But the man who hath naught in his purse is unkind to his family and is disloyal to his king for his own heart is bitter.

"Therefore, the man who wisheth to achieve must have coin that he may keep to jingle in his purse, that he have in his heart love for his family and loyalty to his king."

Second, the PLAN doth provide that I shall support and clothe my good wife who hath returned to me with loyalty from the house of her father. For Mathon doth say that to take good care of a faithful wife putteth self respect into the heart of a man and addeth strength and determination to his purposes.

Therefore seven-tenths of all I earn shall be used to provide a home, clothes to wear, and food to eat, with a bit extra to spend, that our lives be not lacking in pleasure and enjoyment. But he doth further enjoin the greatest care that we spend not greater than seven-tenths of what I earn for these worthy purposes. Herein lieth the success of the PLAN.

I must live upon this portion and never use more nor buy what I may not pay for out of this portion.

TABLET Nº. II

Third, the PLAN doth provide that out of my earnings my debts shall he paid.

Therefore each time the moon is full, two-tenths of all I have earned shall be divided honorably and fairly among those who have trusted me and to whom I am indebted. Thus in due time will all my indebtedness be surely paid.

Therefore, do I here engrave the names of every man to whom I am indebted and the honest amount of my debt.

Fahru, the cloth weaver, 2 silver, 6 copper.

Sinjar, the couch maker, 1 silver.

Ahrnar, my friend, 3 silver, 1 copper.

Zankar, my friend, 4 silver, 7 copper.

Askanir, my friend, 1 silver, 3 copper.

Harinsir, the jewel maker, 6 silver, 2 copper.

Diarbeker, my father's friend, 4 silver, 1 copper.

Alkahad, the house owner, 14 silver.

Mathon, the gold lender, 9 silver.

Birejik, the farmer, 1 silver, 7 copper.

(From here on, disintegrated. Cannot be deciphered.)

TABLET Nº. III

To these creditors do I owe in total one hundred and nineteen pieces of silver and one hundred and forty-one pieces of copper. Because I did owe these sums and saw no way to repay, in my folly I didst permit my wife to return to her father and didst leave my native city and seek easy wealth elsewhere, only to find disaster and to see myself sold into the degradation of slavery.

Now that Mathon doth show me how I can repay my debts in small sums out of my earnings, do I realize the great extent of my folly in running away from the results of my extravagances.

Therefore have I visited my creditors and explained to them that I have no resources which to pay except my ability to earn, and that I intend to apply two-tenths of all I earn upon my indebtedness, evenly and honestly. This much can I pay but no more. Therefore if they be patient, in time my obligations will be paid in full.

Ahmar, whom I thought my best friend, reviled me bitterly and I left him in humiliation. Birejik, the farmer, pleaded that I pay him first as he didst badly need help. Alkahad, the house-owner, was indeed disagreeable and insisted that he would make me trouble unless I didst soon settle in full with him.

All the rest willingly accepted my proposal. Therefore am I more determined than ever to carry through, being convinced that it is easier to pay one's just debts than to avoid them. Even though I cannot meet the needs and demands of a few of my creditors I will deal impartially with all.

TABLET Nº. IV

Again the moon shines full. I have worked hard with a free mind. My good wife hath supported my intentions to pay my creditors. Because of our wise determination, I have earned during the past moon, buying camels of sound wind and good legs, for Nebatur, the sum of nineteen pieces of silver.

This I have divided according to the PLAN. One-tenth have I set aside to keep as my own, seven-tenths have I divided with my good wife to pay for our living. Two-tenths have I divided among my creditors as evenly as could be done in coppers.

I did not see Ahmar but left it with his wife. Birejik was so pleased he would kiss my hand. Old Alkahad alone was grouchy and said I must pay faster. To which I replied that if I were permitted to be well fed and not worried, that alone would enable me to pay faster. All the others thanked me and spoke well of my efforts.

Therefore, at the end of one moon, my indebtedness is reduced by almost four pieces of silver and I possess almost two pieces of silver besides, upon which no man hath claim. My heart is lighter than it hath been for a long time.

Again the moon shines full. I have worked hard but with poor success. Few camels have I been able to buy. Only eleven pieces of silver have I earned. Nevertheless my good wife and I have stood by the plan even though we have bought no new raiment and eaten little but herbs. Again I paid ourselves one-tenth of the eleven pieces, while we lived upon seven-tenths. I was surprised when Ahmar commended my payment, even though small. So did Birejik. Alkahad flew into a rage but when told to give back his portion if he did not wish it, he became reconciled. The others as before were content.

Again the moon shines full and I am greatly rejoiced. I intercepted a fine herd of camels and bought many sound ones, therefore my earnings were forty-two pieces of silver. This moon my wife and myself have bought much needed sandals and raiment. Also we have dined well on meat and fowl.

More than eight pieces of silver we have paid to our creditors. Even Alkahad did not protest.

Great is the PLAN for it leadeth us out of debt and giveth us wealth which is ours to keep.

Three times the moon hath been full since I last carved upon this clay. Each time I paid to myself one-tenth of all I earned. Each time my good wife and I have lived upon seven-tenths even though at times it was difficult. Each time have I paid to my creditors two-tenths. In my purse I now have twenty-one pieces of silver that is mine. It maketh my head to stand straight upon my shoulders and maketh me proud to walk among my friends.

My wife keepeth well our home and is becomingly gowned. We are happy to live together.

The PLAN is of untold value. Hath it not made an honorable man of an ex-slave.

TABLET Nº. V

Again the moon shines full and I remember that it is long since I carved upon the clay. Twelve moons in truth have come and gone. But this day I will not neglect my record because upon this day I have paid the last of my debts. This is the day upon which my good wife and my thankful self celebrate with great feasting that our determination hath been achieved.

Many things occurred upon my final visit to my creditors that I shall long remember. Ahmar begged my forgiveness for his unkind words and said that I was one of all others he most desired for a friend.

Old Alkahad is not so bad after all, for he said. "Thou wert once a piece of soft clay to be pressed and moulded by any hand that touched thee, but thou now art a piece of bronze capable of holding an edge. If thou needst silver or gold at any time come to me."

Nor is he the only man who holdeth me in high regard. Many others speak deferentially to me. My good wife looketh upon me with a light in her eyes that doth make a man have confidence in himself.

Yet it is the PLAN that hath made my success. It hath enabled me to pay all my debts and to jingle both gold and silver in my purse. I do commend it to all who wish to get ahead. For truly if it will enable an ex-slave to pay his debts and have gold in his purse, will it not aid any man to find independence? Nor am I, myself, finished with it, for I am convinced that if I follow it further it will make me rich among men.

ST. SWITHIN'S COLLEGE
NOTTINGHAM UNIVERSITY
NEWARK-ON-TRENT
NOTTINGHAM

November 7th, 1936

Professor Franklin Caldwell,
Care of British Scientific Expedition,
Hillah, Mesopotamia

My dear professor:

If, in your further digging into those bally ruins of Babylon, you encounter the ghost of a former resident, an old camel trader named Dabasir, do me a favor. Tell him that his scribbling upon those clay tablets, so long ago, has earned for him the life long gratitude of couple of college folks back here in England.

You will possibly remember my writing a year ago that Mrs. Shrewsbury and myself intended to try his plan for getting out of debt and at the same time having gold to jingle. You may have guessed, even though we tried to keep from our friends, our desperate straits.

We were frightfully humiliated for years by a lot of old debts and worried sick for fear some of the tradespeople might start a scandal that would force me out of the college. We paid and paid – every shilling we could squeeze out of income, but it was hardly enough to hold things even. Besides we were forced to do all our buying where we could get further credit regardless of higher costs.

It developed into one of those vicious circles that grow worse instead of better. Our struggles were getting hopeless. We could not move to less costly rooms because we owed the landlord. There did not appear to be anything we could do to improve our situation.

Then, here comes your acquaintance, the old camel trader from Babylon, with a plan to do just what we wished to accomplish. He jolly well stirred us up to follow his system. We made a list of all our debts and I took it around and showed it to every one we owed.

I explained how it was simply impossible for me to ever pay them the way things were going along. They could readily see this themselves from the figures. Then I explained that the only way I saw to pay in full was to set aside twenty percent of my income each month to be divided pro rata, which would pay them in full in a little over two years; that, in the meantime, we would go on a cash basis and give them the further benefit of our cash purchases.

They were really quite decent. Our green grocer, a wise old chap, put it in a way that helped to bring around the rest. "If you pay for all you buy and then pay some on what you owe, that is better than you have done, for ye ain't paid down the account none in three years."

Finally I secured all their names to an agreement binding them not to molest us as long as the twenty per cent of income was paid regularly. Then we began scheming on how to live upon seventy per cent. We were determined to keep that extra ten per cent to jingle. The thought of silver and possibly gold was most alluring.

It was like having an adventure to make the change. We enjoyed figuring this way and that, to live comfortably upon that remaining seventy per cent. Started with rent and managed to secure a fair reduction. Next we put our favorite brands of tea and such under suspicion and were agreeably surprised how often we could purchase superior qualities at less cost.

It is too long a story for a letter but anyhow it did not prove difficult. We managed and right cheerfully at that. What a relief it proved to have our affairs in such a shape we were no longer persecuted by past due accounts.

I must not neglect, however, to tell you about that extra ten percent we were supposed to jingle. Well, we did jingle it for some time. Now don't laugh too soon. You see, that is the sporty part. It is the real fun, to start accumulating money that you do not want to spend. There is more pleasure in running up such a surplus than there could be in spending it.

After we had jingled to our hearts content, we found a more profitable use for it. We took up an investment upon which we could pay that ten per cent each month. This is proving to be the most satisfying part of our regeneration. It is the first thing we pay out of my check.

There is a most gratifying sense of security to know our investment is growing steadily. By the time my teaching days are over it should be a snug sum, large enough so the income will take care of us from then on.

All this out of my same old check. Difficult to believe, yet absolutely true. All our old debts being gradually paid and at the same time our investment increasing. Besides we get along, financially, even better than before. Who would believe there could be such a difference in results between following a financial plan and just drifting along?

At the end of the next year, when all our old bills shall have been paid, we will have more to pay upon our investment besides some extra for travel. We are determined never again to permit our living expenses to exceed seventy percent of our income.

Now you can understand why we would like to extend our personal thanks to that old chap whose plan saved us from our 'Hell on Earth', DEBTS.

He knew. He had been through it all He wanted others to benefit from his own bitter experiences. That is why he spent tedious hours carving his message upon the clay.

He had a real message for fellow sufferers, a message so important that after five thousand years it has risen out of the ruins of Babylon, just as true and just as vital as the day it was buried.

Yours sincerely,
Alfred H. Shrewsbury,
Department of Archaeology.

Historical Sketch of Babylon

THE WINGED BULL OF BABYLON
Symbolizing
The Intelligence of Man
The Speed of the Bird
The Strength of the Bull

In the pages of history, there lives no city more glamorous than Babylon. Its very name conjures visions of wealth and splendor. Its treasures of gold and jewels were fabulous. One naturally pictures such a wealthy city as located in a suitable setting of tropical luxuriance, surrounded by rich natural resources of forests and mines. Such was not the case. It was located beside the Euphrates River, in a flat, arid valley. It had no forests, no mine, not even stone for building. It was not even located upon a natural trade route. The rainfall was insufficient to raise crops.

Babylon is an outstanding example of man's ability to achieve great objectives, using whatever means are at his disposal. All of the resources supporting this large city were man developed. All of its riches were man made.

Babylon possessed just two natural resources – a fertile soil and water in the river. With one of the greatest engineering accomplishments of this or any other day, Babylonian engineers diverted the waters from the river by means of dams and immense irrigation canals. Far out across that arid valley went these canals to pour the life giving waters over the fertile soil. This ranks among the first engineering feats known to history. Such abundant crops as were the reward of this irrigation system here, we doubt if the world had ever seen before.

Fortunately, during its long existence, Babylon was ruled by successive lines of kings to whom conquest and plunder were but incidental. While it engaged in many wars, most of these were local or defensive against ambitious conquerors from other countries who coveted the fabulous "Treasures of Babylon". The outstanding rulers of Babylon live in history because of their wisdom, enterprise and justice. Babylon produced no strutting monarchs who sought to conquer the known world that all nations might pay homage to their egotism.

As a city, Babylon exists no more. When those energizing human forces that built and maintained the city for thousands of years, were withdrawn, it soon became

91

a deserted ruin. The site of the city is in Asia about six hundred miles east of the Suez Canal, just north of the Persian Gulf. The latitude is about 30 degrees above the Equator, practically the same as that of Yuma, Arizona. It possessed a climate similar to that of this American city, hot and dry.

Today, this valley of the Euphrates, once a populous irrigated farming district, is again the wind swept arid waste. Scant grass and desert shrubs strive for existence against the wind blown sands. Gone are the fertile fields, the mammoth cities and the long caravans of rich merchandise. Nomadic bands of Arabs, securing a scant living by tending small herds are the only inhabitants. Such it has been since about the beginning of the Christian era.

Dotting this valley are earthen hills. For centuries, they were considered by travelers to be nothing else. The attention of archaeologists was finally attracted to them because of pieces of pottery and brick washed down by the occasional rain storms. Expeditions, financed by European and American Museums, were sent here to excavate and see what could be found. Picks and shovels soon proved these hills to be ancient cities. City graves, they might well be called.

Babylon was one of these. Over it for something like twenty centuries, the winds had scattered the desert dust. Built originally of brick, all exposed walls had disintegrated and gone back to earth once more. Such is Babylon, the wealthy city, today. A heap of dirt, so long abandoned that no living person even knew its name until it was discovered by carefully removing the refuse of centuries from the streets and the fallen wreckage of its noble temples and palaces.

Many scientists consider the civilization of Babylon and other cities in this valley to be the oldest of which there is a definite record. Positive dates have been proved reaching back 8000 years. An interesting fact in this connection is the means used to determine these dates. Uncovered in the ruins of Babylon, were descriptions of an eclipse of the sun. Modern astronomers readily computed the time when such an eclipse, visible in Babylon, occurred and thus established a known relationship between their calendar and our own.

In this way, we have proved that 8000 years ago the Sumerites, who inhabited Babylonia, were living in walled cities. One can only conjecture for how many centuries previous such cities had existed. Their inhabitants were not mere barbarians living within protecting walls. They were an educated and enlightened people. So far as written history goes, they were the first engineers, the first astronomers, the first mathematicians, the first financiers and the first people to have a written language.

Mention has already been made of the irrigation systems which transformed the arid valley into an agricultural paradise. The remains of these canals can still be traced, although they are mostly filled with accumulated sand. Some of them were of such size that, when empty of water, a dozen horses could be ridden along their bottoms abreast. In size they compare favorably with the largest canals in Colorado and Utah.

In addition to irrigating the valley lands, Babylonian engineers completed another project of similar magnitude. By means of an elaborate drainage system they reclaimed an immense area of swamp land at the mouths of the Euphrates and Tigris Rivers and put this also under cultivation.

Herodotus, the Greek traveler and historian, visited Babylon while it was in its prime and has given us the only known description by an outsider. His writings give a graphic description of the city and some of the unusual customs of its people. He mentions the remarkable fertility of the soil and the bountiful harvests of wheat and barley which they produced.

The glory of Babylon has faded but its wisdom has been preserved for us. For this we are indebted to their form of records. In that distant day, the use of paper had not been invented. Instead, they laboriously engraved their writing upon tablets of moist clay. When completed, these were baked and became hard tile. In size, they were about six by eight inches and an inch in thickness.

These day tablets, as they are commonly called, were used much as we use modem forms of writing. Upon them were engraved lengthy legends, rare poetry, history, transcriptions of royal decrees, the laws of the lands, titles to property, promissory notes and even letters which were dispatched by messengers to distant cities. From these day tablets we are permitted an insight into the intimate personal affairs of the people. For example, one tablet, evidently from the records of a country storekeeper, relates that upon the given date a certain named customer brought in a cow and exchanged it for seven sacks of wheat, three being delivered at the time and the other four to await the customer's pleasure.

Another gives a part of the autobiography of Ashurbanipal, one of their kings. Among other things, he advises us: "The beautiful writing in Sumerian, that is difficult to remember, it was my joy to repeat. I directed the weaving of reed shields and breastworks like a pioneer. I had the learning that all clerks of every kind possess when their time of maturity comes. At the same time I learned what is proper for lordship."

Safely buried in the wrecked cities, archaeologists have recovered entire libraries of these tablets, hundreds of thousands of them.

Of the outstanding wonders of Babylon were the immense walls surrounding the city. The ancients ranked them with the great pyramid of Egypt, as belonging to the "Seven Wonders of the world". Queen Semiramis is credited with having erected the first walls during the early history of the city. Modern excavators have been unable to find any trace of the original walls. Nor is their exact height known. From mention made by early writers, it is estimated they were about fifty to sixty feet high, faced on the outer side with burned brick and further protected by a deep moat of water.

The later and more famous walls were started about six hundred years before the time of Christ by King Nabopolassar. Upon such a gigantic scale did he plan the rebuilding, he did not live to see the work finished. This was left to his son, Nebuchadnezzar, whose name is familiar in Biblical history.

The height and length of these later walls staggers belief. They are reported upon reliable authority to have been about one hundred and sixty feet high, the equivalent of the height of a modern fifteen story office building. The total length is estimated as between nine and eleven miles. So wide was the top, that a six-horse chariot could be driven around them. Of this tremendous structure, little now remains except portions of the foundations and the moat. In addition to the ravages of the elements, the Arabs completed the destruction by quarrying the brick for building purposes elsewhere.

Against the walls of Babylon marched, in turn, the victorious armies of almost every victorious conqueror of that age of wars of conquest. A host of kings laid siege to Babylon, but always in vain. Invading armies of that day were not to be considered lightly. Historians speak of such units as 10,000 horsemen, 25,000 chariots, 1200 regiments of foot soldiers with 1000 men to the regiment. Often two to three years of preparation would be required to assemble war materials and depots of food along the proposed line of march.

The city of Babylon was organized much like a modem city. There were streets and shops. Peddlers offered their wares through residential districts. Priests officiated in magnificent temples. Within the city was an inner enclosure for the royal palaces. The walls about this were said to have been higher than those about the city.

The Babylonians were skilled in the arts. These included sculpture, painting, weaving, gold working and the manufacture of metal weapons and agricultural implements. Their jewelers created most artistic jewelry. Many samples have been recovered from the graves of its wealthy citizens and are now on exhibition in the leading museums of the world.

At a very early period when the rest of world was still hacking at trees with stone headed axes, or hunting and fighting with flint pointed spears and arrows, the Babylonians were using axes, spears and arrows with metal heads.

The Babylonians were clever financiers and traders. So far as we know, they were the original inventors of money as a means of exchange, of promissory notes and written titles to property.

Babylon was never entered by hostile armies until about 540 years before the birth of Christ. Even then the walls were not captured. The story of the fall of Babylon is most unusual. Cyrus, one of the great conquerors of that period, intended to attack the city and hoped to take its impregnable walls. Advisors of Nabonidus, the King of Babylon, persuaded him to go forth to meet Cyrus and give him battle without waiting for the city to be besieged.

In the succeeding battle Cyrus administered such an astounding defeat to the Babylonian army, it fled away from the city. Cyrus, thereupon, entered the open gates and took possession without resistance.

Thereafter the power and prestige of the city gradually waned until, in the course of a few hundred years, it was eventually abandoned, deserted, left for the winds and storm to level once again to that desert earth from which its grandeur had originally been built. Babylon had fallen, never to rise again, but to it civilization owes much.

The eons of time have crumbled to dust the proud walls of its temples, but the wisdom of Babylon endureth.

THE MAGIC STORY

by
Frederick Van Rensselaer Day

An immediate, **worldwide** sensation was created after "The Magic Story" first made its appearance in **1900** in the original 'Success' Magazine. After 1000's of requests for the reprint, a tiny, silver book was published. The story is presented here so that you too may benefit from its powerful message.

The book is in two parts. Part 1 below reveals the story of Sturtevant, a starving artist who's life was changed overnight after he purchased an old, ragged scrapbook for 3 cents. Within the scrapbook he found what he said was a "magic story". **Everyone** he told the story to prospered by it. It seemed to change people's lives for the better like magic. Part 2 on the next page is the **actual** Magic Story as found by Sturtevant.

The Magic Story - Part 1

How the Magic Story was found....

I was sitting alone in the cafe and had just reached for the sugar preparatory to putting it into my coffee. Outside, the weather was hideous. Snow and sleet came swirling down, and the wind howled frightfully. Every time the outer door opened, a draft of unwelcome air penetrated the uttermost corners of the room. Still I was comfortable.

The snow and sleet and wind conveyed nothing to me except an abstract thanksgiving that I was where it could not affect me. While I dreamed and sipped my coffee, the door opened and closed, and admitted - Sturtevant. Sturtevant was an undeniable failure, but, withal, an artist of more than ordinary talent. He had, however, fallen into the rut traveled by ne'er-do-wells, and was out at the elbows as well as insolvent.

As I raised my eyes to Sturtevant's I was conscious of mild surprise at the change in his appearance. Yet he was not dressed differently. He wore the same threadbare coat in which he always appeared, and the old brown hat was the same. And yet there was something new and strange in his appearance. As he swished his hat around to relieve it of the burden of snow dposited by the howling nor'wester, there was something new in the gesticulation.

I could not remember when I had invited Sturtevant to dine with me, but involuntarily I beckoned to him. He nodded and presently seated himself opposite to me. I asked him what he would have, and he, after scanning the bill of fare carelessly, ordered from it leisurely, and invited me to join him in coffee for two.

I watched him in stupid wonder, but, as I had invited the obligation, I was prepared to pay for it, although I knew I hadn't sufficient cash to settle the bill. Meanwhile I noticed the brightness of his usual lackluster eyes, and the healthful, hopeful glow upon his cheek, with increasing amazement.

"Have you lost a rich uncle?" I asked. "No," he replied, calmly, "but I have found my mascot." "Brindle, bull or terrier?" I inquired. "Currier," said Sturtevant, at length, pausing with his coffee cup half way to his lips, "I see that I have surprised you. It is not strange, for I am a surprise to myself. I am a new man, a different man, - and the alteration has taken place in the last few hours.

You have seen me come into this place 'broke' many a time, when you have turned away, so that I would think you did not see me. I knew why you did that.

It was not because you did not want to pay for a dinner, but because you did not have the money to do it. Is that your check? Let me have it. Thank you. I haven't any money with me tonight, but I, - well, this is my treat." He called the waiter to him, and, with an inimitable flourish, signed his name on the backs of the two checks, and waved him away.

After that he was silent for a moment while he looked into my eyes, smiling at the astonishment which I in vain strove to conceal. "Do you know an artist who possess more talent than I?" he asked, presently. "No. Do you happen to know anything in the line of my profession that I could not accomplish, if I applied myself to it? No. You have been a reporter for the dailies for - how many? - seven or eight years. Do you remember when I ever had any credit until tonight? No. Was I refused just now? You have seen for yourself. Tomorrow my new career begins. Within a month I shall have a bank account. Why? Because I have discovered the secret of success." "Yes," he continued, when I did not reply, "my fortune is made. I have been reading a strange story, and since reading it, I feel that my fortune is assured. It will make your fortune, too. All you have to do is read it. You have no idea what it will do for you. Nothing is impossible after you know that story. It makes everything as plain as A, B, C. The very instant you grasp its true meaning, success is certain. This morning I was a hopeless, aimless bit of garbage in the metropolitan ash can; tonight I wouldn't change places with a millionaire. That sounds foolish, but it is true. The millionaire has spent his enthusiasm; mine is all at hand."

"You amaze me," I said, wondering if he had been drinking absinthe.

"Won't you tell me the story? I should like to hear it."

"Certainly. I mean to tell it to the whole world. It is really remarkable that it should have been written and should remain in print so long, with never a soul to appreciate it until now. This morning I was starving. I hadn't any credit, nor a place to get a meal. I was seriously meditating suicide.

I had gone to three of the papers for which I had done work, and had been handed back all that I had submitted. I had to choose quickly between death by suicide and death slowly by starvation. Then I found the story and read it. you can hardly imagine the transformation. Why, my dear boy, everything changed at once, - and there you are."

"But what is the story, Sturtevant?"

"Wait; let me finish. I took those old drawings to other editors, and every one of them was accepted at once." "Can the story do for others what it has done for you? For example, would it be of assistance to me?" I asked. "Help you? Why not? Listen and I will tell it to you, although, really, you should read it. Still I will tell it as best I can. It is like this: you see, - - -" The waiter interrupted us at that moment. He informed Sturtevant that he was wanted on the telephone, and with a word of apology, the artist left the table.

Five minutes later I saw him rush out into the sleet and wind and disappear. Within the recollection of the frequenters of that cafe, Sturtevant had never before been called out by telephone. that, of itself, was substantial proof of a change in his circumstances.

One night, on the street, I encountered Avery, a former college chum, then a reporter on one of the evening papers. It was about a month after my memorable interview with Sturtevant, which, by that time, was almost forgotten. "Hello, old chap," he said; "how's the world using you? Still on space?" "Yes," I replied, bitterly, "with prospects of being on the town, shortly. But you look as if things were coming your way. Tell me all about it."

"Things have been coming my way, for a fact, and it is all remarkable, when all is said. You know Sturtevant, don't you? It's all due to him. I was plumb down on my luck, - thinking of the morgue and all that, - looking for you, in fact, with the idea you would lend me enough to pay my room rent, when I met Sturtevant. He told me a story, and, really, old man, it is the most remarkable story you ever heard; it made a new man out of me. Within twenty-four hours I was on my feet and I've hardly known a care or a trouble since."

Avery's statement, uttered calmly, and with the air of one who had merely pronounced an axiom, recalled to my mind the conversation with Sturtevant in the cafe that stormy night, nearly a month before. "It must be a remarkable story," I said, increduously. "Sturtevant mentioned it to me once. I have not seen him since. Where is he now?" "He has been making war sketches in Cuba, at two hundred a week; he's just returned. It is a fact that everybody who has heard the story has done well since. There are Cosgrove and Phillips, - friends of mine, - you don't know them. One's a real estate agent; the other's a broker's clerk, Sturtevant told them the story, and they have experienced the same results that I have; and they are not the only ones.

"Do you know the story?" I asked. "Will you try its effect on me?" "Certainly; with the greatest pleasure in the world. I would like to have it printed in big black type, and posted on the elevated stations throughout New York. It certainly would do a lot of good, and it's as simple as A, B, C: like living on a farm. Excuse me a minute, will you? I see Danforth over there. Back in a minute, old chap." If the truth be told, I was hungry. My pocket at that moment contained exactly five cents; just enough to pay my fare up-town, but insufficient also to stand the expense of filling my stomach.

There was a "night owl" wagon in the neighborhood, where I had frequently "stood up" the purveyor of midnight dainties, and to him I applied. He was leaving the wagon as I was on the point of entering it, and I accosted him. "I'm broke again," I said, with extreme cordiality. "You'll have to trust me once more. Some ham and eggs, I think, will do for the present." He coughed, hesitated a moment, and then re-entered the wagon with me. "Mr. Currier is good for anything he orders'" he said to the man in charge; "one of my old customers. This is Mr. Bryan, Mr. Currier. He will take good care of you, and 'stand for' you, just the same as I would. The fact is, I have sold out. I've just turned over the outfit to Bryan. By the way, isn't Mr. Sturtevant a friend of yours?" I nodded.

I couldn't have spoken if I had tried. "Well," continued the ex-"night owl" man, "he came in here one night, about a month ago, and told me the most wonderful story I ever heard. I've just bought a place in Eighth Avenue, where I am going to run a regular restaurant - near Twenty-third Street. Come and see me." He was out of the wagon and the sliding door had been banged shut before I could stop him; so I ate my ham and eggs in silence, and resolved that I would hear that story before I slept. In fact, I began to regard it with superstition.

If it had made so many fortunes, surely it should be capable of making mine. The certainty that the wonderful story - I began to regard it as magic - was in the air, possessed me. As I started to walk homeward, fingering the solitary nickel in my pocket and contemplating the certainty of riding downtown in the morning, I experienced the sensation of something stealthily puruing me, as if Fate were treading along behind me, yet never overtaking, and I was conscious that I was possessd with or by the story.

When I reached Union Square, I examined my address book for the home of Sturtevant. It was not recorded there. Then I remembered the cafe in University Place, and, although the hour was late, it occured to me that he might be there. He was! In a far corner of the room, surrounded by a group of acquaintences, I saw him. He discovered me at the same instant, and motioned to me to join them at the table. There was no chance for the story, however. There were half a dozen around the table, and I was the furthest removed from Sturtevant. But I kept my eyes upon him, and bided my time, determined that, when he rose to depart, I would go with him.

A silence, suggestive of respectful awe, had fallen upon the party when I took my seat. Everyone had seemed to be thinking, and the attention of all was fixed upon Sturtevant. The cause was apparent. He had been telling the story. I had entered the cafe just too late to hear it. On my right, when I took my seat, was a doctor; on my left a lawyer. Facing me on the other side was a novelist with whom I had some acquaintance. The others were artists and newspaper men.

"It's too bad, Mr. Currier," remarked the doctor; "you should have come a little sooner, Sturtevant has been telling us a story; it is quite wonderfuil, really. I say, Sturtevant, won't you tell that story again, for the benefit of Mr. Currier?" "Why yes. I believe that Currier has, somehow, failed to hear the magic story, although, as a matter of fact, I think he was the first one to whom I mentioned it at all. It was here, in this cafe, too, -at this very table.

Do you remember what a wild night that was, Currier? Wasn't I called to the telephone, or something like that? To be sure! I remember, now; interrupted just at the point when I was beginning the story. After that I told it to three or four fellows, and it 'braced them up,' as it had me. It seems incredible that a mere story can have such a tonic effect upon the success of so many persons who are engaged in such widely different occupations, but that is what it has done. It is a kind of never-failing remedy, like a cough mixture that is warranted to cure everything, from a cold in the head to galloping consumption. There was Parsons, for example. He is a broker, you know, and had been on the wrong side of the market for a month. He had utterly lost his grip, and was on the verge of failure. I happened to meet him at the time he was feeling the bluest, and before we parted, something brought me around to the subject of the story, and I related it to him. It had the same effect on him as it had on me, and has had on everybody who has heard it, as far as I know.

I think you will all agree with me, that it is not the story itself that performs the surgical operation on the minds of those who are familiar with it; it is the way it is told, -in print, I mean. The author has, somehow, produced a psychological effect which is indescribable. The reader is hypnotized. He receives a mental and moral tonic.

Perhaps, doctor, you can give some scientific explanation of the influence exerted by the story. It is a sort of elixir manufactured out of words, eh?" From that the company entered upon a general discussion of theories. Now and then slight references were made to the story itself, and they were just sufficient to tantalize me - the only one present who had not heard it.

At length, I left my chair, and passing around the table, seized Sturtevant by one arm, and succeeded in drawing him away from the party. "If you have any consideration for an old friend who is rapidly being driven mad by the existence of that confounded story, which Fate seems determined that I shall never hear, you will relate it to me now," I said, savagely. Sturtevant stared at me in wild surprise. "All right," he said. "The others will excuse me for a few moments, I think. Sit down here, and you shall have it. I found it pasted in an old scrapbook I purchased in Ann Street, for three cents and there isn't a thing about it by which one can get any idea in what publication it originally appeared, or who wrote it. When I discovered it, I began casually to read it, and in a moment I was interested. Before I left it, I had read it through many times, so that I could repeat it almost word for word. It affected me strangely, -as if I had come in contact with some strong personality.

There seems to be in the story a personal element that applies to every one who reads it. Well, after I had read it several times, I began to think it over. I couldn't stay in the house, so I seized my coat and hat and went out. I must have walked several miles, bouyantly, without realizing that I was the same man, who, in only a short time before, had been in the depths of despondency. That was the day I met you here, -you remember." We were interrupted at that instant by a uniformed messenger, who handed Sturtevant a telegram. It was from his chief, and demanded his instant attendance at the office. The sender had already been delayed an hour, and there was no help for it; he must go at once. "Too bad!" said Sturtevant, rising and extending his hand.

"Tell you what I'll do, old chap. I'm not likely to be gone any more than an hour or two. You take my key and wait for me in my room. In the escritoire near the window you will find an old scrapbook bound in rawhide. It was manufactured, I have no doubt, by the author of the magic story. Wait for me in my room until I return."

I found the book without difficulty. It was a quaint, home-made affair, covered, as Sturtevant had said, with rawhide, and bound with leather thongs. The pages formed an odd combination of yellow paper, vellum and homemade parchment. I found the story, curiously printed on the last-named material. It was quaint and strange. Evidently, the printer had "set" it under the supervision of the writer. The phraseology was an unusual combination of seventeenth and eighteenth century mannerisms, and the interpolation of italics and capitals could have originated in no other brain than that of its author. In reproducing the following story, the peculiarities of type, etc. are eliminated, but in other respects it remains unchanged.

The Magic Story - Part 2
by
Unknown Author

Inasmuch as I have evolved from my experience the one great secret of success for all worldly undertakings, I deem it wise, now that the number of my days is nearly counted, to give to the generations that are to follow me the benefit of whatsoever knowledge I possess. I do not apologize for the manner of my expression, nor for the lack of literary merit, the latter being, I wot, its own apology. Tools much heavier than the pen have been my portion, and moreover, the weight of years has somewhat palsied the hand and brain; nevertheless, the fact I can tell, and what I deem the meat within the nut. What mattereth it, in what manner the shell be broken, so that the meat be obtained and rendered useful? I doubt not that I shall use, in the telling, expressions that have clung to my memory since childhood; for, when men attain the number of my years, happenings of youth are like to be clearer to their perceptions than are events of recent date; nor doth it matter much how a thought is expressed, if it be wholesome and helpful, and findeth the understanding.

Much have I wearied my brain anent the question, how best to describe this recipe for success that I have discovered, and it seemeth advisable to give it as it came to me; that is, if I relate somewhat of the story of my life, the directions for agglomerating the substances, and supplying the seasoning for the accomplishment of the dish, will plainly be perceived. Happen they may; and that men may be born generations after I am dust, who will live to bless me for the words I write.

My father, then, was a seafaring man who, early in life, forsook his vocation, and settled on a plantation in the colony of Virginia, where, some years thereafter, I was born, which event took place in the year 1642; and that was over a hundred years ago. Better for my father had it been, had he hearkened to the wise advice of my mother, that he remain in the calling of his education; but he would not have it so, and the good vessel he captained was bartered for the land I spoke of. Here beginneth the first lesson to be aquired:

Man should not be blinded to whatsoever merit exists in the opportunity which he hath in hand, remembering that a thousand promises for the future should weigh as naught against the possession of a single piece of silver.

When I had achieved ten years, my mother's soul took flight, and two years thereafter my worthy father followed her. I, being their only begotten, was left alone; howbeit, there were friends who, for a time, cared for me; that is to say, they offered me a home beneath their roof, - a thing which I took advantage of for the space of five months. From my father's estate there came to me naught; but, in the wisdom that came with increasing years, I convinced myself that his friend, under whose roof I lingered for some time, had defrauded him, and therefore me.

Of the time from the age of twelve and a half until I was three and twenty, I will make no recital here, since that time hath naught to do with this tale; but some time after, having in my possession the sum of sixteen guineas, ten, which I had saved from the fruits of my labor, I took ship to Boston town, where I began to work first as a cooper, and thereafter as a ship's carpenter, although always after the craft was docked; for the sea was not amongst my desires.

Fortune will sometimes smile upon an intended victim because of pure perversity of temper. Such was one of my experiences. I prospered, and at seven and twenty, owned the yard wherein, less than four years earlier, I had worked for hire. Fortune, howbeit, is a jade who must be coerced; she will not be coddled. Here beginneth the second lesson to be acquired:

Fortune is ever elusive, and can only be re- tained by force. Deal with her tenderly and she will forsake you for a stronger man. (In that, me- thinks, she is not unlike other women of my knowledge.)

About this time, Disaster (which is one of the heralds of broken spirits and lost resolve), paid me a visit. Fire ravaged my yards, leaving me nothing in its blackened paths but debts, which I had not the coin wherewith to defray. I labored with my acquaintances, seeking assistance for a new start, but the fire that had burned my competence, seemed also to have consumed their sympathies. So it happened, within a short time, that not only had I lost all, but I was hopelessly indebted to others; and for that they cast me into prison. It is possible that I might have rallied from my losses but for this last indignity, which broke down my spirits so that I became utterly despondent. Upward of a year I was detained within the gaol; and, when I did come forth, it was not the same hopeful, happy man, content with his lot, and with confidence in the world and its people, who had entered there.

Life has many pathways, and of them by far the greater number lead downward. Some are precipitous, others are less abrupt; but ultimately, no matter at what inclination the angle may be fixed, they arrive at the same destination - failure. And here beginneth the third lesson:

Failure exists only in the grave. Man, being alive, hath not yet failed; always he may turn about and ascend by the same path he descended by; and there may be one that is less abrupt (albeit longer of achievement), and more adaptable to his condition.

When I came forth from prison, I was penniless. In all the world I possessed naught beyond the poor garments which covered me, and a walking stick which the turnkey had permitted me to retain, since it was worthless. Being a skilled workman, howbeit, I speedily found employment at good wages; but, having eaten of the fruit of worldly advantage, dissatis-faction possessed me. I became morose and sullen; whereat, to cheer my spirits, and for the sake of forgetting the losses I had sustained, I passed my evenings at the tavern. Not that I drank overmuch of liquor, except on occasion (for I have ever been somewhat abstemious), but that I could laugh and sing, and parry wit and badinage with my ne'er-do-well companions; and here might be included the fourth lesson:

Seek comrades among the industrious, for those who are idle will sap your energies from you.

It was my pleasure at that time to relate, upon slight provocation, the tale of my disasters, and to rail against the men whom I deemed to have wronged me, because they had seen fit not to come to my aid. Moreover, I found childish delight in filching from my employer, each day, a few moments of the time for which he paid me. Such a thing is less honest than downright theft. This habit continued and grew upon me until the day dawned which found me not only without employment, but also without character, which meant that I could not hope to find work with any other employer in Boston town.

It was then that I regarded myself a failure. I can liken my condition at that time for naught more similar than that of a man who, descending the steep side of a mountain, loses his foothold. The farther he slides, the faster he goes. I have also heard this condition described by the word Ishmaelite, which I understand to be a man whose hand is against everybody, and who thinks that the hands of every other man are against him; and here beginneth the fifth lesson:

The Ishmaelite and the leper are the same, since both are abominations in the sight of man, - albeit they differ much, in that the former may be restored to perfect health. The former is entirely the result of imagination; the latter has poison in his blood.

I will not discourse at length upon the gradual degeneration of my energies. It is not meet ever to dwell much upon misfortunes (which saying is also worthy of remembrance). It is enough if I add that the day came where I possessed naught wherewith to purchase food and raiment, and I found myself like unto a pauper, save at infrequent times when I could earn a few pence, or mayhap, a shilling. Steady employment I could not secure, so I became emanciated in body, and naught but skeleton in spirit.

My condition, then, was deplorable; not so much for the body, be it said, as for the mental part of me, which was sick unto death. In my imagination I deemed myself ostracized by the whole world, for I had sunk very low indeed; and here beginneth the sixth and final lesson to be acquired, (which cannot be told in one sentence, nor in one paragraph, but must needs be adopted from the remainder of this tale).

Well do I remember my awakening, for it came in the night, when, in truth, I did awake from sleep. My bed was a pile of shavings in the rear of the cooper shop where once I had worked for hire; my roof was the pyramid of casks, underneath which I had established myself. The night was cold, and I was chilled, albeit, paradoxically, I had been dreaming of light and warmth and of the depletion of good things. You will say, when I relate the effect the vision had on me, that my mind was affected. So be it, for it is the hope that the minds of others might be likewise influenced which disposes me to undertake the labor of this writing. It was the dream which converted me to the belief - nay, to the knowledge - that I was possessed of two entities: and it was my own better self that afforded me the assistance for which I had pleaded in vain from my acquaintances. I have heard this condition described by the word "double." Nevertheless, that word does not comprehend my meaning. A double, can be naught more than a double, neither half being possessed of individuality. But I will not philosophize, since philosophy is naught but a suit of garments for the decoration of a dummy figure.

Moreover, it was not the dream itself which affected me; it was the impression made by it, and the influence that it exerted over me, which accomplished my enfranchisement. In a word, then, I encouraged my other identity. After toiling through a tempest of snow and wind, I peered into a window and saw that other being. He was rosy with health; before him, on the hearth, blazed a fire of logs; there was a conscious power and force in his demeanor; he was phisically and mentally muscular. I rapped timidly upon the door, and he bade me enter. There was a not unkindly smile of derision in his eyes as he motioned me to a chair by the fire; but he uttered no word of welcome; and, when I had warmed myself, I went forth again into the tempest, burdened with the shame which the contrast between us had forced upon me. It was then that I awoke; and here cometh the strange part of my tale, for, when I did awake, I was not alone. There was a Presence with me; intangible to others, I discovered later, but real to me.

The Presence was in my likeness, yet it was strikingly unlike. The brow, not more lofty than my own, yet seemed more round and full; the eyes, clear, direct, and filled with purpose, glowed with enthusiasm and resolution; the lips, chin, - ay, the whole contour of face and figure was dominant and determined. He was calm, steadfast, and self-reliant; I was cowering, filled with nervous trembling, and fearsome of intangible shadows. When the Presence turned away, I followed, and throughout the day I never lost sight of it, save when it disappeared for a time beyond some doorway where I dared not enter; at such places, I awaited its return with trepidation and awe, for I could not help wondering at the temerity of the Presence (so like myself, and yet so unlike), in daring to enter where my own feet feared to tread.

It seemed also as if purposely, I was led to the place and to the men where, and before whom I most dreaded to appear; to offices where once I had transacted business; to men whith whom I had financial dealings. Throughout the day I pursued the Presence, and at evening saw it disappear beyond the portals of a hostelry famous for its cheer and good living. I sought the pyramid of casks and shavings.

Not again in my dreams that night did I encounter the Better Self (for that is what I have named it), albeit, when, perchance, I awakened from slumber, it was near to me, ever wearing that calm smile of kindly derision which could not be mistaken for pity, nor for condolence in any form. The contempt of it stung me sorely.

The second day was not unlike the first, being a repetition of its forerunner, and I was again doomed to wait outside during the visits which the Presence paid to places where I fain would have gone had I possessed the requesite courage. It is fear which deporteth a man's soul from his body and rendereth it a thing to be despised. Many a time I essayed to address it but enunciation rattled in my throat, unintelligible; and the day closed like its predecessor.

This happened many days, one following another, until I ceased to count them; albeit, I discovered that constant association with the Presence was producing an effect on me; and one night when I awoke among the casks and discerned that he was present, I made bold to speak, albeit with marked timidity. "Who are you?" I ventured to ask; and I was startled into an upright posture by the sound of my own voice; and the question seemed to give pleasure to my companion, so that I fancied there was less of derision in his smile when he responded.

"I am that I am," was the reply. "I am he who you have been; I am he who you may be again; wherefore do you hesitate? I am he who you were, and whom you have cast out for other company. I am the man made in the image of God, who once possessed your body. Once we dwelt within it together, not in harmony, for that can never be, nor yet in unity, for that is impossible, but as tenants in common who rarely fought for full possession. Then, you were a puny thing, but you became selfish and exacting until I could no longer abide with you, therefore I stepped out. There is a plus-entity and minus-entity in every human body that is born into the world. Whichever one of these is favored by the flesh becomes dominant; then is the other inclined to abandon its habitation, temporarily or for all time. I am the plus-entity of yourself; you are the minus-entity. I own all things; you possess naught. That body which we both inhabited is mine, but it is unclean, and I will not dwell within it. Cleanse it, and I will take possession."

"Why do you pursue me?" I next asked of the Presence. "You have pursued me, not I you. You can exist without me for a time, but your path leads downward, and the end is death. Now that you approach the end, you debate if it be not politic that you should cleanse your house and invite me to enter. Step aside, from the brain and the will; cleanse them of your presence; only on that condition will I ever occupy them again."

"The brain has lost its power," I faltered. "The will is a weak thing, now; can you repair them?"

"Listen!" said the Presence, and he towered over me while I cowered abjectly at his feet. "To the plus-entity of a man, all things are possible. The world belongs to him, - is his estate. He fears naught, dreads naught, stops at naught; he asks no privileges, but demands them; he dominates, and cannot cringe; his requests are orders; opposition flees at his approach; he levels mountains, fills in vales, and travels on an even plane where stumbling is unknown."

Thereafter, I slept again, and, when I awoke, I seemed to be in a different world. The sun was shining and I was conscious that birds twittered above my head. My body, yesterday trembling and uncertain, had become vigorous and filled with energy. I gazed upon the pyramid of casks in amazement that I had so long made use of it for an abiding place, and I was wonderingly conscious that I had passed my last night beneath its shelter.

The events of the night recurred to me, and I looked about me for the Presence. It was not visble, but anon I discovered, cowering in a far corner of my resting place, a puny abject shuddering figure, distorted of visage, deformed of shape, disheveled and unkept of appearance. It tottered as it walked, for it approached me piteously; but I laughed aloud, mercilessly. Perchance I knew then that it was the minus-entity, and that the plus-entity was within me; albeit I did not then realize it. Moreover, I was in haste to get away; I had no time for philosophy. There was much for me to do, - much; strange it was that I had not thought of that yeaterday. But yesterday was gone, - today was with me, - it had just begun.

As had once been my daily habit, I turned my steps in the direction of the tavern, where formerly I had partaken of my meals. I nodded cheerily as I entered, and smiled in recognition of returned salutations. Men who had ignored me for months bowed graciously when I passed them on the thoroughfare. I went to the washroom, and from there to the breakfast table; afterwards, when I passed the taproom, I paused a moment and said to the landlord:

"I will occupy the same room that I formerly used, if perchance, you have it at disposal. If not, another will do as well, until I can obtain it."

Then I went out and hurried with all haste to the cooperage. There was a huge wain in the yard, and men were loading it with casks for shipment. I asked no questions, but, seizing barrels, began hurling them to the men who worked atop of the load. When this was finished, I entered the shop. There was a vacant bench; I recognized its disuse by the litter on its top. It was the same at which I had once worked. Stripping off my coat, I soon cleared it of impedimenta. In a moment more I was seated, with my foot on the vice-lever, shaving staves.

It was an hour later when the master workman entered the room, and he paused in surprise at sight of me; already there was a goodly pile of neatly shaven staves beside me, for in those days I was an excellent workman; there was none better, but, alas! now, age hath deprived me of my skill. I replied to his unasked question with the brief, but comprehensive sentence: "I have returned to work, sir." He nodded his head and passed on, viewing the work of other men, albeit anon he glanced askance in my direction.

Here endeth the sixth and last lesson to be aquired, although there is more to be said, since from that moment I was a successful man, and ere long possessed another shipyard, and had acquired a full competence of worldly goods.

I pray you who read, heed well the following admonitions, since upon them depend the word "success" and all that it implies:

Whatsoever you desire of good is yours. You have but to stretch forth your hand and take it.

Learn that the consciousness of dominant power within you is the possession of all things attainable. *Have no fear* of any sort or shape, for fear is an adjunct of the minus-entity. If you have skill, apply it; the world must profit by it, and therefore, you. Make a daily and nightly companion of your plus-entity; if you heed its advice, you cannot go wrong.

Remember, philosophy is an argument; the world, which is your property, is an accumulation of facts. Go therefore, and do that which is within you to do; take no heed of gestures which would beckon you aside; *ask of no man permission to perform.*

The minus-entity requests favors; the plus-entity grants them. Fortune waits upon every footstep you take; seize her, bind her, hold her, for she is yours; she belongs to you.

Start out now, with these admonitions in your mind. Stretch out your hand, and grasp the plus, which, maybe, you have never made use of, save in great emergencies. Life is an emergency most grave.
Your plus-entity is beside you now; cleanse your brain, and strengthen your will. It will take possession. It waits upon you. *Start tonight; start now upon this new journey.* Be always on your guard. Whichever entity controls you, the other hovers at your side; beware lest the evil enter, even for a moment.

My task is done. I have written the recipe for "success." If followed, it cannot fail. Wherein I may not be entirely comprehended, the plus-entity of whosoever reads will supply the deficiency; and upon that Better Self of mine, I place the burden of imparting to generations that are to come, the secret of this all-pervading good, -the secret of being what you have it within you to be.

THE END

Recommended Readings

- Riches Are Your Right by Joseph Murphy

- How To Win Friends And Influence People: A Condensation From The Book by Dale Carnegie

- How to Make a Fortune Today-Starting from Scratch: Nickerson's New Real Estate Guide by William Nickerson

- Praying the Psalms by Thomas Merton

- The Magic of Believing by Claude M. Bristol

- Scientific Advertising by Claude C. Hopkins

- The Law of Success: Using the Power of Spirit to Create Health, Prosperity, and Happiness by Paramahansa Yogananda

- How I Learned the Secrets of Success in Selling by Frank Bettger

- You Can Still Make It In The Market by Nicolas Darvas

Available at www.bnpublishing.com